LIVING
ON THE LEVEL

LIVING
ON THE LEVEL

ONE-STORY HOUSES
BY ROYAL BARRY WILLS

HOUGHTON MIFFLIN COMPANY BOSTON
THE RIVERSIDE PRESS CAMBRIDGE · 1955

The Riverside Press · CAMBRIDGE, MASSACHUSETTS

Printed in the U.S.A.

ACKNOWLEDGMENTS

The author wishes to express his appreciation

to his associates

MERTON S. BARROWS and ROBERT E. MINOT

whose intelligent efforts contributed much to

the planning of the houses shown herein.

Thanks are due to Leon Keach for his able assistance

in editing the text and also to Charles Crombie

for the beautiful execution of many of

the finished drawings.

The house on the cover is that of

Mr. and Mrs. B. F. Kraus, Falmouth, Massachusetts.

CONTENTS

ARCHITECTS ARE PEOPLE too, and they vary between wide extremes in their opinions as to what kind of houses should be built to satisfy the needs of today's family. The axis of their philosophies extends from that of the insistently radical modernist and International stylist on the one hand to that of the obstinately determined traditionalist on the other, with Frank Lloyd Wright and his followers maintaining a sternly held position away from and at right angles to the line connecting the two. Small wonder that there is confusion in the mind of the average citizen confronting the problem of how best to spend the sizable chunk of money necessary to pay for a permanent shelter. Fortunately there is a mid-position in which the majority may find solace, mindful of the possible validity today of Pope's famous couplet, "Be not the first by whom the new are tried, Nor yet the last to lay the old aside."

We happen to believe that a man or woman has a right to choose the sort of living environment he or she wants to set up to shelter a family. We recognize the merit that lies in all the serious design thought that goes into good houses of all persuasions, both conservative and radical, and we conceive it to be our duty as architects to understand the whys and wherefores that brought them into being.

The amount and quality of the thinking that goes into the planning of your house makes all the difference in its convenience; the knowledge and experience back of the decisions that have to be made about its materials and methods of construction determine its structural soundness and resistance to the weather; the degree of sensibility to beauty possessed by its designer and by yourself limit the amount of pleasure you will experience while you live in it. So get the best advice you can find on these things and be true to yourself if you want to be completely happy in your home.

It is the purpose of this book to provide you with information that will be of use to you, ideas that may help you to save money, and examples of good design that should help you to decide what sort of house appeals to your particular mental and spiritual individuality.

PART ONE

PAST IMPERFECT AND FUTURE CONDITIONAL

WE AND OUR FELLOW ARCHITECTS have known troubled years within the profession, during which any zealously proclaimed theory of architectural design could be matched by another, much at odds with it but no less forcefully sponsored.

Whatever the excesses of the late lamented Eclectic Period it gave vast impetus to a study of the world's architectural heritage, an impressive panorama that lay shimmering and undisturbed for many a decade. In retrospect perhaps we didn't know how privileged we were; time was when the limits of one's artistic appreciation were quite circumscribed by the arbiters of the moment, who alone thought they knew the truth, and the monuments of a past age served as mere stone quarries for the next one. It was a blow for freedom, if not for cultism, that we were allowed to review the whole field unmolested.

The better architects who selected and designed from this ocean of varied inspiration ranged from the fundamentalist to the liberal; some of them could create a "period" house correct to the half hour, while others stirred in enough original thinking to remove the design even from a "style" tag, let alone "period." It was generally observed that their product was hailed as either a step towards a new architecture or just the awful result of defying conventions. But even as a pleasant life, a benign outlook and a full stomach make a poor breeding ground for iconoclastic movements, so it took a great war and a demoralized world finally to produce a pure and self-perpetuating revolutionary strain.

With the advent of architectural modernism, out of Europe in the twenties, we again witnessed a closed world in the making, marked by the inevitable intolerance and certitude of prescription that suggested direct revelation. This compulsion for total change as reflected in plan, material and structural treatment, even in the delineation of its documents, forced the acceptance of an aesthetic impoverishment which has not yet wholly been sloughed off. When beauty, as she was understood for a few thousand years, was foresworn and her empty niche filled by a figure made of bent chromed pipes, called "functionalism," we were not completely convinced.

Things just had to be that way, for some inscrutable reason, but it's too bad, for the Wahabits always had a case of sorts. There was the onrushing world of changing social patterns and technological advances, a natural for new solutions, but with freshness tempered by humility. As an example of how rudely we "old contemptibles" were shaken by the Teutonic onslaught, let us consider the matter of material selection. For years no architect with a sense of responsibility for his clients' money would specify a piece of equipment or a material that had not been tried out by others and found satisfactory. Of necessity the fiercely forward looking new movement clove to new materials, on the ecstatic recommendation of salesmen, and to startling and often illogical uses of familiar ones. When something went sour, as it frequently did, the conservative onlooker could not but feel that the needless disregard for sound practice was inexcusable. This was the superimposed "shoebox phase" with flat roof and stucco wall, the time of the unlovely pipe column, fir flooring used vertically as an outside wall, and the colorless, clinical look.

Those of us who were following the main

stream of architecture viewed this new movement with even more annoyance than we did that of the classical cultists. We didn't like it because it denied much of the validity of previous experience and subjected middle-road progress to ridicule, while it was doing some patently ridiculous things itself. Then there was a feeling that a congeries of fads, masquerading as the Word, was being shoved down one's throat.

In the fullness of time three events came along to give strength to the cause of modernist planning: the disappearance of household help, the rising cost of construction, and the age of mechanical gadgetry. The first called for an immediate revision of house design, as we shall see later, and the last, seeming to complement the first, gave a specious virtue to a contemporary housing for the machines. The second, with house dimensions growing ever smaller as costs increased, made a case for the open plan with its illusion of greater space.

Admittedly there were always points of interest in contemporary thought, but when projected to their full solution even by practitioners of the greatest skill, we had a recurring conviction that the nub of this or that idea could be softened and improved in a more traditionalist setting. That leaven began its work some years ago and has led us to embrace a position in the architectural order of things which some may call eclectic, though to our mind humanist is a fairer term. We see no virtue in strict adherence to any cult whose tenets deny the worth of other schools of thought, when all, being human, may very well have made gross errors or achieved successes. Short of the above-mentioned direct revelation it is the individual and no high priest who must decide what is good and true.

So we say we like a mixture of traditional and contemporary architecture, a culling of the latter's crisp reassessment of the house plan but girded with some of the warmth and beauty of the past. Of course we realize that this sounds a little like the office seeker who called himself a progressive-conservative, or the auctioneer selling late Early American antiques. We might even have to risk being dubbed a modern-

traditionalist, but we've got to take the chance. There is artistic sensibility as well as modernist sense to be considered; fun as well as function. Simplicity in decorative design is here to stay, if only because of high prices, but there is no reason for making a fetish of austerity, for neglecting color, humor, for not encouraging a little silliness now and then, even being downright impractical at some point, just to break the monotony. We like changing patterns of light and shade on a whitewashed brick wall. Foolish to paint brick—well, maybe. We like very narrow clapboards, natural in color. It's a little wasteful but the effect of soft striation is worth a few dollars as an aesthetic pleasure.

To be functional, an organization of rooms and services does not have to affect a barren asepticism. When the ultimate objective of pure functionalism was made to supplant traditional function with beauty it had, of course, to presume an entirely new concept of beauty as that phenomenon disclosed by functionalism *per se*. This was a piece of stage business and it served its purpose, though at appalling cost. It needn't have been propounded, as we think we are proving today with houses which assuredly function in a mid-century manner, are warm, colorful, yet express their structure and purpose forthrightly, at the same time being relaxed and regionally appropriate.

Nevertheless, as the contemporary years pass, it sometimes seems as though beauty again had her foot in the door and might come to share her old niche with functionalism, perhaps using the chromed pipes as a chair. Even a Wahabit can't blind himself to the charm of natural materials forever.

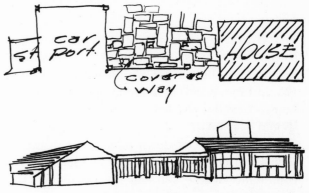

See how big this makes the little house look.

3

With air conditioning you can use fixed glass windows. Big savings — no vents — no screens.

Fixed Glass

We have examined the growth of heliolatry, as expressed through glass walls, the predilection for high strip-windows on certain façades, and we agree fully, with the stipulation that circumstances alter cases. There seems to be no ponderable benefit to the health through admitting large amounts of daylight, any more than there is when the average person takes vitamins in tablet form; one gets enough of both in ordinary, conservative living. But if there is a view of some quality or a subscription to the fad of sun worship we have a good case for the glass wall, in places where it does not destroy necessary privacy. To be at one with nature in one's living room may be an exhilarating experience, but we would not care to be at one with U.S. Route 1, or Neighbor Updike's back yard. High strip-windows give privacy, wall space and high ventilation, but many uninhibited people and specialists in claustrophobia have an aversion to them, with no regard for their standing as a contemporary device. In short, we would *not* say that a house just had to have big windows, or high ones either, to look well or to live well; it is a matter of location and personal preference.

The Spartan period of modern architecture has passed its apogee relative to the world of historical precedent and already shows a life-nourishing warmth in some hands. Though the twain may never meet they have greatly influenced one another, and to their mutual benefit.

With a form of mass production growing in the building industry a great step has been taken to swing this last stand of individualized hand assembly over into the big time. As a matter of housing economics it figures as a victory and will be so recognized by thousands of young married Americans eager to get a roof over their heads at minimum cost.

There will be less enthusiasm among thoughtful architects, both contemporary and traditional, whose sense of social values is not too strong and untempered to blind them to the evils as well as the advantages of mass production. In this rather late stand for the retention of some trace of the individual will, some expression of the special wishes or needs of a family, both traditional and contemporary architects will find themselves in the same army, a fact that would have seemed unbelievable twenty years ago.

NOTES ON PUTTING THE RIGHT FOOT FORWARD

IT HATH BEEN SAID that renting is cheaper than owning, and that if you want the maximum amount of shelter for the least money you should buy an old, obsolete nineteenth century house. Granted the truth of these two rumors, should you own?

If you like to put down roots and cultivate a social and economic stability, an identity in a community where you can raise a family, the principle of house ownership is excellent.

When you buy the shelter needed for your family, the 1880 model in a slightly passé neighborhood gives you a lot more cubage per dollar. Perhaps it's old and grey and full of leaks and ready for a series of major repairs, but if you can tackle them one by one the mere fact of solvency is preserved.

When you elect to build it may not be because you have a corpulent wallet so much as a long-nourished wish to live in new, up-to-date quarters. Or you may have been thwarted in shaping a way of life by the unyielding obsolescence of some stout, high-posted old ark, where the silent undulations of a ceiling cobweb were almost out of broom's reach. Perhaps a trailer park convinced you that your zest for camping had evaporated and you'd give your shirt for a little privacy in a well-designed house. It could be that the astonishing and limitless offerings of the magazines, or the new possession of a friend, sold you an idea, or maybe you won a give-away program jackpot and had to have an up-to-date place to store the gear (even a niche for the Geiger counter). Whatever the motive there are the same steps to be taken.

When you're going for new construction there are at least four ways to take the plunge:

(a) to buy a speculative house.

(b) to order a house of similar antecedents from a speculative builder, for a set price.

(c) to buy stock plans and hire a builder.

(d) to hire an architect or a designer and let him plan and supervise the construction of your house.

Schemes (a) and (b) are sometimes all that could be asked for and result in a satisfied customer who knows at once the immediate cost of getting a roof over him and his family. But there is a greater theoretical risk even if all is outwardly satisfactory, because you are accepting the assembly of a complicated structure on the supposition of honest work.

In normal times speculative builders are dealing in a most inflexible and chancy product, definitely risky, and their history is fraught with disaster. It is their proper hope to make a profit on land and house, and generous enough to warrant the risk involved. They start with a bank loan, perhaps at an upped rate due to inherent uncertainties, and have to face a broker's fee, taxes, insurance, legal fees, etc., over and above their costs for lot and construction. The cost of plans is inconsiderable because they use the same ones repeatedly. As a house is held for sale over a period of time the taxes and maintenance costs must be added to its purchase price if possible, or the profit dwindles. Altogether, if he's lucky, you may

A simple wood screen can make all the difference between privacy and the lack of it. This one shields terrace from kitchen door.

get $7,500.00 worth of house, exclusive of land cost, for every $10,000.00 you spend, leaving $2,500.00 as the builder's profit for relieving you of the trouble of having it built.

The success of scheme (c) is dependent upon several things:

(a) Besides suiting your needs the plan must fit the lot or have revision costs added.

(b) You have got to know materials and mechanical devices or accept the opinion of interested parties.

(c) Landscape problems may not be included in the plans, and don't forget screens, shades and the like.

(d) You must avoid changing your mind and incurring extras.

(e) You should *know* your builder, for so much depends upon his integrity.

In fine, unless the builder is one of those sterling characters of our acquaintance, though they don't abound, you have assumed a sizable burden and risk for the purpose of saving money over the employment of an architect.

The hiring of a capable professional, an architect or in some cases a designer, because the difficulty of getting registered keeps many able men from the full title of "architect," should obviate a host of uncertainties. Their fee covers their costs and profit. In $10,000.00 worth of house the latter may be about $1,000.00. Even with other costs incidental to construction (insurance, etc.) at least a tenth more of your money should be applied to construction, *and under an architect's supervision*, than obtains through dealing with a speculative builder. If under those positive safeguards you don't get quite the amount of space and equipment that you would have by buying a speculative house there is a very good reason, and it concerns the higher cost of better methods.

When you're going to build and have a lot that has passed the general fitness test you may check further with a qualified and disinterested person, an architect for instance. You may pretty well rest assured that, even if he expects to get a job out of it, he will render a fair judgment. The difficulties of a poor lot and your unending lament over troubles resulting therefrom should insure probity in the analysis. It is a very different matter when you ask the advice of a real estate agent who is trying to unload the property.

The purchase of land involves two documents, a *deed* or legal evidence of the transaction, and a *title*, which is the legal proof that the seller owns the land completely with no strings attached. A lawyer must check the validity of the title before you pay for your real estate. If you are applying for an immediate construction loan the bank will check the title for its own protection (and charge you for it) so there would be no need for having anyone else do it.

Builders can count on no major repairs for years, but builders *and* buyers have immediate decisions as to whether or no they can pay for the accommodations they have got to have. If the full or ultimate program is distinctly out, consider one or two steps, perhaps three. This isn't the way to achieve the lowest final cost, but it is one way of providing yourself with a house that can grow with your own financial resources.

You'll have a down payment, and a mortgage to amortize over a period of years, present assets limiting the one and earning power enabling the other. No guess or general rule elicits the facts at this point as well as an orderly recording of your credits and debits. Even though an officer in your chosen bank is a potentially interested person he has reason to want a successful transaction, so may be of help on the knotty question as to what is safe to spend. He should have a good idea concerning the relation of that sum to the cost of the program you have in mind. Even if the two balance up you have got to have your plans approved before being sure you will receive the mortgage.

Until recently, and even now to some extent, it has not been easy to interest Eastern lending institutions in contemporary houses, purely because in this transitional period there are many people who think they dislike them. And if there is anything a banker abhors more than a robber it's a house on his hands that nobody wants to buy.

In excess of the cost of the land and the amount of the mortgage there are the inevitable legal fees and charges, to make you marvel at the intricacies of life and part with a couple hundred dollars, more or less. Of this minor expense the cost of a survey is well worth while and the rest is at least according to law or custom.

GETTING A LOT FOR YOUR MONEY

WHETHER YOU ARE SEEKING to build in the country, the suburbs or the suburban fringe, the following points will evoke pertinent questions and information to guide you.

GENERAL AREA SELECTION

A. *Neighbors*—In quitting the easy anonymity of apartment living for the identity of house ownership, motives to guide one towards selection of a site should be kept as practical as possible with an eye to the long economic, educational and social haul. But the initial attraction seems to be: (a) a convenient location; (b) nearby friends; (c) an attractive countryside or, (d) a congenial community. There can be no recommendation on this point except to

Pick a lot with loam on it and sell the loam.

suggest that the fact of a contented ownership usually entails one's identification with an agreeable society of like pecuniary status and general outlook. If the pace is too expensive or the group incompatible the relative permanence of one's ownership begets a misery.

B. *Schools*—In rural areas the public schools may be indifferent and hardly capable of booting the average student into college. This also happens in some manufacturing centers with unusually marked gap between the limits of personal wealth. The affluent whose business keeps the town going, send their children to private schools and have no interest in supporting the public school system, though it would be difficult to find one who would verify that point.

C. *Medical*—City dwellers will want to know just how thin the doctors are spread in outlying areas. Also, how far away is the nearest reputable hospital?

D. *Services*—Of obvious interest to both parents. In a single bath dwelling, when little Charlotte tries to flush one of her sister's diapers down the watercloset and there is an overflow, it is very convenient to have a plumber reasonably near. So, too, when the oil heater breaks down on a winter's night. If you shouldn't shovel snow and your boy's too young, someone else or a machine has got to do the work.

E. *Local Government*—Even small communities get to be strangled by entrenched low-grade politicians. Discover if a comparatively heavy construction program is about to be launched—schools, sewers, roads—and if the town has an aversion to bond issues, preferring to raise taxes as high as necessary. The policy of assessing is of interest, on high or low valuations, and reputedly there are places where, if you keep the front lawn trimmed and plant a few shrubs to decorate the foreparts, the assessors reward you for your good work with a slight tax upping.

F. *Public Services*—Well drilling is fraught with some uncertainty but the successes greatly outnumber the expensive failures. Usually the artesian output is more than ample for family use, and after it has been analyzed, its hard or soft characteristics determined and an electric pump and a storage tank installed, you give it no further thought.

There is no uncertainty about a septic tank, if it is properly designed in relation to family size and the normal water-level of surrounding land, plus soil conditions. With existing services somewhere in the vicinity there is the initial check as to how far the municipality will go towards making them available and how much more than the normal bill you will have to foot.

Incinerators and garbage disposers overcome everything but the riddance to tins and bottles, so some removal service is a necessity, the more so if your septic tank finds life a little hard with a disposer taxing it.

The quality of the perhaps never needed services of the local fire department and police department is usually disregarded, even though when they are wanted the need is dire. It may be argued that half the nation would still be a wilderness if the citizenry was conservative on this point.

G. *Utilities and Transportation*—In case light and power rates are pretty reasonable and you are tempted by the thought of an all-electric house, be sure to have a good fireplace or a camp stove to fall back on for heat and cooking when the power fails in bad weather, as it surely will, albeit briefly and rarely. Piped-in or bottled gas has a better record on this score (as long as you remember to keep a filled bottle).

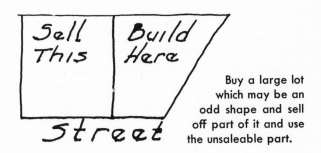

Buy a large lot which may be an odd shape and sell off part of it and use the unsaleable part.

7

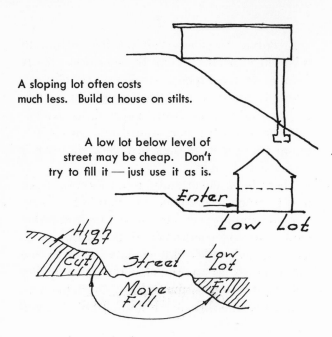

A sloping lot often costs much less. Build a house on stilts.

A low lot below level of street may be cheap. Don't try to fill it — just use it as is.

Buy a lot cheap because it's low. Buy a lot across the street cheap because it's high. Then fill the low lot from the high lot and sell one lot for a good price.

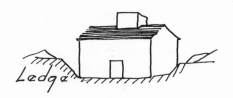

A ledgy lot may be cheap. Just build around the ledge.

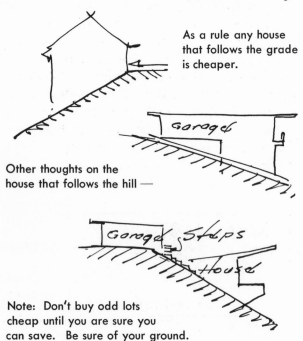

As a rule any house that follows the grade is cheaper.

Other thoughts on the house that follows the hill —

Note: Don't buy odd lots cheap until you are sure you can save. Be sure of your ground.

Buy a big lot with an old house on it and sell the old house for the actual cost and keep a lot.

Public transportation grows worse by the minute and the lack of it may be an itch for commutors or one-car families. A matter for serious thought.

H. *Shopping Centers*—Here is a matter of such immediacy that it cannot possibly be overlooked by the lady of the house, whose normal buying procedure will determine her reaction to what she finds in a new location. The lord of the manor should remember that when the beer gives out of a summer evening in a no-license town it may be serious.

I. *Recreation*—Playgrounds may not be necessary but a supervised place for skating is important, as is some organization for adolescent team games. Adult clubs are of value or not, as you view them, but 4H, Campfire or Scout groups serve a good purpose.

THE LOT ITSELF

To imagine the ideal lay of a small lot, it should face northwards to the road and have the living room and its grounds to the south. Countless millions have lived happily with just the opposite arrangement, because they didn't know it was wrong, or perhaps it doesn't make too much difference to the average person.

Though the sun is greatly desirable in living quarters most of the year, an even greater feature to many people is a pleasant outward prospect. The prevailing wind for summer cooling is a third consideration and the architect strives to catch the best features of all three. In a small lot the added fact of sloping land pretty well complicates this endeavor, and dictates the lay of the house. Usually its length follows the contour and it has a single story on one side, two on the other. A gentle slope up from the road is most favorable.

ARCHITECTURAL CHARGES are usually based on a schedule evolved by professional organizations and issued in the form of a blue book. The book's fees are not intended to be mandatory, but rather to be indicative of what the profession regards as adequate, under normal conditions, for the performance of architectural services.

The scope of full services includes:

(a) Preliminary study of the problem, with tentative sketches.

(b) Basic drawings and outline specifications on which to get a preliminary estimate of costs.

(c) Working drawings, including some basic details, and detailed specifications, which become the contract documents and upon which is based the contractor's estimate.

(d) Contract letting, further details, review of all bills submitted by the contractor, regular inspection of the work, guidance in the selection of mechanical equipment, finishes, fixtures, colors, hardware, and so forth.

The range is sufficiently comprehensive so that an owner could take a leisurely trip round the world and leave his personal representative, the architect, to defend his interests and execute the project.

For these services the architect's only recompense is his fee, and about one fifth of that is his profit; the rest is absorbed by his own overhead. In contrast, the contractor stands to make money on his contractual estimate by economy in purchasing materials and by skill and good timing in pursuing his construction. In addition to which he receives a clear profit of ten per cent (or thereabouts) on the cost of all the work he does.

Another attribute of the architect which can-

not be assumed by the builder or contractor, the real estate man or the lumberyard, is the feeling for design, the ability to put grace, beauty and good scale into a building so that it is something more than a neat, well mechanized lump. His profession spans the gulf between the creative imagination and the most practical of building problems.

The task of selecting an architect is often a poser for a person nourishing a building problem that needs resolving. There should be a little thought and investigation before taking the plunge. Many practitioners have a variety of building types to their credit; some concentrate on one or a very few types. The tendency of the times in architecture, as in so many other fields, is for specialization. This may be unfortunate but it does breed expertness, which is an extra dividend for the client. All structures, like all machines, gain steadily in complexity as the years pass, and this abets the

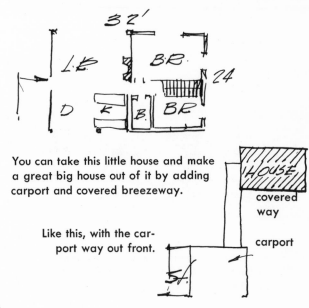

You can take this little house and make a great big house out of it by adding carport and covered breezeway.

Like this, with the carport way out front.

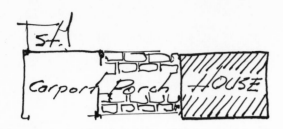

This looks big. Makes a structure about 70 feet long.

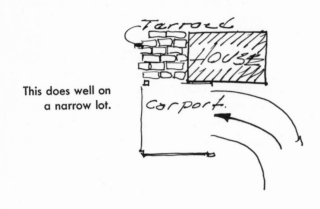

This does well on a narrow lot.

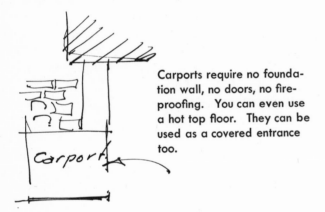

Carports require no foundation wall, no doors, no fireproofing. You can even use a hot top floor. They can be used as a covered entrance too.

If you turn carport opening sideways to street and build one side solid or for storage wall, you can screen the interior which is never too neat.

specialist; in fact many building committees insist on him as Item No. 1.

Past clients have positive ideas on an architect's worth, but you have got to take an average between the overenthusiastic friend and the crank. Check on the building and on business and contract procedure, the quality of supervision.

When an architect has to add a strange contractor to a list of bidders he telephones fellow professionals until he finds a number who have done business with him. He checks on the man's skill and honesty, on his ability to work satisfactorily in a specific price range, and his business standing in the trade. A report may label him as reliable and conscientious, but it is necessary to watch his subcontractors. This implies that the contractor will produce the low figure you need through picking subcontractors who will take work at a small profit, but you will have a constant fight to hold them to the standards of your specifications and drawings.

Ask about extras. They are charges over and above the contract figure for work not covered by the working drawings and specifications. They may arise from two causes, an error of omission by the architect or a change of mind by the client. It is bad handling not to keep the latter constantly apprised of each one when it arises, of its cost and of the accumulated cost of past extras.

Make sure that when the architect does your purchasing and gets a professional discount you receive its benefit; remember that the professional receives no gratuities in excess of his fee. A recent occurrence comes to mind where a client, in ignorance of regular procedure, dealt directly with a high-pressure salesman for an expensive kitchen. Had she worked through the architect he might well have talked her out of the extravagance, but if unsuccessful at least he could have turned back about a thousand dollars, which would have been his discount on the purchases.

The principal in a busy office cannot possibly hope to know the details of every job. That is the business of his assistants, who actually make the drawings and are responsible for the exact information. A sheet-metal subcontractor once told me that when he found a general contractor laying bricks on the job he got the pay for his metal work as quickly as possible, for he knew that a principal thus tying himself up in a trade detail was not long for this solvent world; he was correct.

Although an architect with much on his mind has no time for specific details he does control the design of every important item by reviewing each drawing before it is issued for printing. On routine telephone calls to an office you can get more direct information on details by asking for the man who is running the job. He has the exact data in mind and may make minor decisions without having to refer them to his boss.

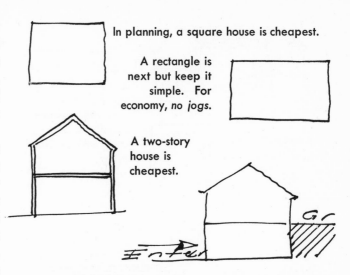

In planning, a square house is cheapest.

A rectangle is next but keep it simple. For economy, *no jogs*.

A two-story house is cheapest.

A house set in the bank combines benefits of two-story and one-story.

THE ADVANTAGES OF LIVING ON THE LEVEL

SUMMER TRIPPERS THROUGH BRITAIN and the continent have long granted the chill impressiveness of the big manor, the chateau or the great villa, but have reserved their more enthusiastic emotions for the charm of the cottage districts. Most Americans would find life in these delightful little houses a bit sticky, especially where they tripped over free-roaming hens and pet porkers. But of course that thought really doesn't concern them for it is the scale, with its snug storybook flavor, that beguiles. A scale, incidentally, which is only attainable in the one-story house, *if* it is well designed.

It is no accident that led us first to mention the exterior excellence of our subject. We all know that the plan's the thing and that a perfect exterior cannot compensate for a bad plan. Yet there is never any excuse for letting a dull, uninspired exterior clothe a good plan. Certainly it cannot be argued that a livable plan is bound to result in external merit; that's just too good to be true.

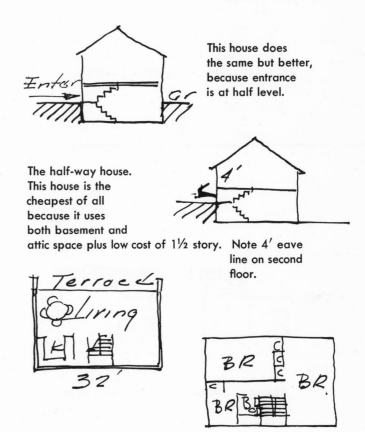

This house does the same but better, because entrance is at half level.

The half-way house. This house is the cheapest of all because it uses both basement and attic space plus low cost of 1½ story.

Note 4' eave line on second floor.

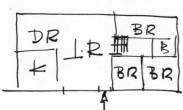

The split level house provides many economies, and also combines benefits of one-story and two-story living.

By utilizing space over garage a lot of extra room is acquired.

A homely but economical way to put a garage in the half-way house.

A better-looking way is to have garage entrance at rear.

This house gives a low look being only 9'–0" from ground to eave. It makes for a lot of living because it opens onto a terrace at first floor in rear.

Since World War II, which opened the era of the one-story house and a vast activity in building, even the most insensitive observer has been appalled at the number of drab structures that have been built. Neither of good traditional nor contemporary design and by no means subsistence-level dwellings, most of them are utterly characterless. The minimum versions have an extra strike against them, because they are already too small and quite inflexible in the event there is any truth in the saying that "the rich get rich and the poor get children."

Granting the esthetic fitness of the one-story house in modern eyes we can, we believe, prove rather conclusively that it may be bent to present day living more perfectly than any other type. Its predominant virtues conserve effort and so make life easier, make a safer house and a more flexible one.

First off let it never be said that for equal living area, in an average plan, a one-story house is exactly as cheap as one of two stories. The difference is often about 7 per cent in the latter's favor, for it requires less land, foundation, roof, insulation; less cost for floors, ceilings, interior partitions, doors and windows.

That the privilege of one-story living is not more costly may be attributed to savings in stairs, shorter plumbing lines and heating ducts, less height of chimney and sidewalls, the lack of staging during construction. There is an inherent benefit in reduction of the cross-grain wood shrinkage that cracks plaster, and many maintenance costs diminish. You are able to make home repairs safely and can even do your own house painting. All bearing partitions may be eliminated by a trussed roof that is carried only on the outer walls, and gives complete freedom for partition changes within the shell of the house. If you have an attic space it will give twice the area for storage offered by a two-story house of similar accommodation.

Although we may argue, and we do, that a step or two more in the kitchen or elsewhere is an unimportant detail if it allows a better overall plan, there is sometimes a curious, latent antipathy towards taking that step or two. When they have the option of an underpass at a busy street crossing, how many people prefer to chance it against the traffic. The few steps down and up are no appreciable effort, but the shorter passage on one plane has an over-riding attraction. Those who live in turn-of-the-century houses are accustomed to five or six steps up from entrance walk to first floor and thirteen to fifteen steps more to the second floor. How many times we need some object upstairs, postpone the getting of it, and then run up two steps at a time when we finally bring ourselves to it.

The almost complete elimination of multiple levels is only part of the attraction in a one-story house, but a psychologically important part, which has factual significance among older people.

Besides catering to our physical inertia or limitations the stairless house saves the housewife many a weary lug; the regular toting up and down of laundry and cleaning gear, the trips up to make beds, the trips down to answer the doorbell. It removes a hazard that is said to account for 25 per cent of household accidents.

Luckily we don't carry our apprehensions far enough to relate a house plan to the broken leg we may come by some day. More often the advantage of one story is in our thoughts when there are old people in the family; then it is important. And, too, there is the factor of safety in the serious event of fire.

Supervision during illness or over young children is apt to be less trouble on one floor, and the house quieter. Noise is difficult to eliminate through floors, much easier to control horizontally. And privacy is not reduced by one level, as the study of a good one-story plan will show.

House for house the low, contour-fitting form of the one level design best fulfills the esthetic and inherent demand for houses that are knit into the landscape. Be it an Umbrian farmhouse, an Austrian chalet or a Cotswold cottage there is the same quality of being completely harmonious with the land.

This feeling of being a part of the scene is an active ingredient in one-story living. To be able to look or step into a garden, to serve meals there, is a privilege we all would enjoy.

The house may embrace its entrance court or a wing may bend to shield a corner for outdoor living, perhaps in conjunction with a fine shade tree, a hedge row or a sapling fence.

The combinations are about limitless and under trained and sympathetic guidance for almost any house program there will be a one-story solution that far surpasses its two-story alternate in appearance and convenience.

On second thought the tent house is the cheapest of all because it uses all low-cost space.

Section through tent house shows low-cost balcony bedroom with ship's ladder stair.

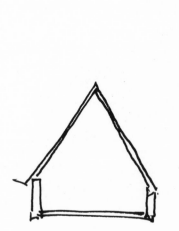 

This tent house roof has a hinge which makes for easy prefabbing and transportation.

Housebuilding is usually contemplated far enough in advance of design and construction for the lady in the case to have accumulated a fairly complete set of preliminary notions as to what she wants. It is inconceivable that she has not made an orderly presentation of her demands as related to her needs. One of the advantages of architectural service should be a clarification and resolution of these matters before design.

The architect doesn't use a couch to elicit this information, in fact family details that do not have a bearing on design are of no importance to him. You might say that it is no concern of the architect if the client beats his wife, unless he has to have a special room for the project or finds his technique is improved by special wall colors.

A device we have used for some years is the client's data sheet. It has undergone revision but strives essentially for a résumé of family and personal details that bear on plan, on design predelictions and on space demands.

Client's Data Sheet

1. Type and proposed cost of building.
2. For permanent occupancy or possible future sale.

Combination kitchen-fireplace and barbecues are all the rage now.

Personal Data

3. Members of family—sex, ages, etc.
4. Probably future additions or possible accretions.
5. Work habits of adults—
   (a) Husband—works away, home office, partially at home.
   (b) Wife—outside activity which may require reflection in plan.
6. Work habits of children—
   (a) Day school and live at home.
   (b) Boarding school.
   (c) Music study.
7. Play habits of adults—
   (a) Social activities — formal, informal, frequency.
   (b) Hobbies.
   (c) Music activity.
8. Play habits of children—
   (a) Games.
   (b) Hobbies or collections.
9. Hired hands, if any—
   (a) Servant—full, part time.
   (b) Cleaning and/or laundering.
   (c) Nursemaid.
   (d) Help during social affairs.
   (e) Outside help on grounds or gardens.
10. Normal routine—
    (a) Degree of disciplining and scheduling in family.
    (b) Traffic tangles in morning use of bath.
    (c) Eating habits—
    Breakfast—kitchen or dining area, together or in stages.
    Luncheon—how many and where.
    Dinner—Degree of formality and size.
    (d) Evening at home—

Need for segregating adult and child activity, a quiet area for adult reading or child study. Place for confining radio or TV.

Design Data

11. Schedule of rooms desired—
    (a) Special relationship between live-work-sleep areas.
    (b) Approximate sizes.
    (c) Special storage.
    (d) Compartmented baths.
12. General character of design—
    (a) Traditional.
    (b) Free indigenous.
    (c) Modern (contemporary open plan).
    (d) Room or rooms for special accent.

Keep away from too many original ideas like trees growing in the living room. They add expense and may cause problems.

13. Furniture—
    (a) Character and amount of furniture on hand.
    (b) Probable future trend in purchases.
14. Dependencies—
    (a) Garage and size.
    (b) Others—summer shelter, tool house, etc.

HE WHO DOES THE BUILDING

THE GENERAL CONTRACTOR is the man who is paid to construct your building, and on whom one places responsibility for co-ordinating and overseeing the various subcontractors who participate in the work.

Architects have doubled as general contractors, but that is a very debatable combination and ethically tabu by the American Institute of Architects.

Contractors are not formally classified like birds, beetles and bandits, of the families Parulidae and Amara or Public Enemy #6, but they fall into a few general classes with a little nudging.

In the beginning there is the handy jack-of-all-trades with vestigial pretensions to a contractor's title, and no liability insurance. He will undertake maintenance and repair work that you might call a general contractor about. Perhaps he's an independent soul who won't work for a g.c. but hasn't business sense enough to make a profitable go of it; perhaps he is an amiable fellow with built in strains of insta-

bility and elbow-bending which don't quite jibe up with the rigors of regular hours. His price is the lowest, but he has no capital to carry the job to a conclusion before billing you, so you will have to buy his materials and pay him at intervals, if the work lasts that long. His selling point is a low rate, his faults, if any, would concern skill, reliability and guaranteed insolvency.

Also in the lone-wolf category, but of a more voracious breed, is the contractor with no organization who is really a broker, for he may not even own a hammer. When undertaking a job he has to sublet all of his work, even carpentry. Although there would appear to be no fundamental reason why this rather infrequent scheme is poor we have some good but more bad records concerning it, which might imply that the broker's own capacity tipped the scales. A good point has been the amount of attention given the job, because usually he only undertakes one at a time. Unfavorably the work has been handled without craft-pride and with

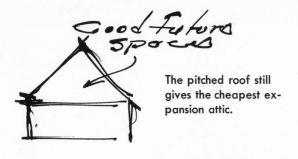

Good future space

The pitched roof still gives the cheapest expansion attic.

Insulate well. Put in a perfect job of insulation and you can heat a house with a candle.

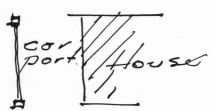

carport / House

Use a carport instead of garage. Side wall may have snowbreak of plywood or fencing.

Use this

or this

Not This

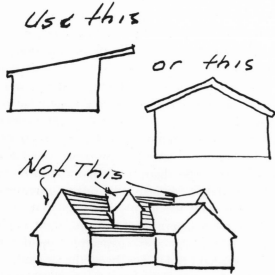

Simple-shaped roofs are cheapest. Avoid multiple gables and complicated roof lines to save cost.

an overriding suggestion that the broker was not close enough to the details of building really to know what it was all about. Whereas this man will carry employees' liability insurance (and charge you for it) the handyman just flies in the face of Providence, so if he is injured in your service you may receive a pecuniary low blow.

Next in order is the small non-union organization of three or four men. Perhaps the contractor boss is a carpenter with two or three others working for him, and with regular connections in the other trades (such as plumbing, masonry, electrical and heating). He will have a small shop to store his gear, a few power tools and a light truck.

Another variety is the family group, sometimes a father and two or three sons. Both these set-ups are apt to submit the lowest estimates of any responsible enough to be entrusted with a building operation, if we exclude the broker. Generalizations are no sooner made than disproved but, to hazard one, they will not produce more than an average result. Even though it meets your specifications to the letter a given detail will not have the finish a first rank craftsman can impart. These fellows are often "silent-type" men, who have a tendency ·when in doubt to use their not always gifted imaginations instead of calling up the architect. Letter writing is poison to them.

Moving up a notch, there is what seems to be the average contracting organization, carrying a number of union carpenters and laborers, owning a woodworking shop, having an office with a secretary, and with a number of trucks. Here is the first appearance of a recognizable business organization and with a reassuring permanency. Contractors with much of an invested stake in the business are apt to be tenacious and in it for keeps. There will be experienced carpenters and the foreman carpenter, or job boss, is more often than not a very capable overlord who enforces standards of workmanship that redound to honest construction. Subcontractors will be chosen with a higher regard for skill, letters will be exchanged in normal fashion, and the contractor will demand (and receive) detailed drawings

16

before proceeding with the work. He has at least as good imagination as the smaller operator but lacks the other's blissful aloofness from the tyranny of drawn or written records.

Of course you will have to pay more for his services and they are worth more. In the better instances, for there are gradations of excellence in all groups, both architect and client have complete assurance that there will be no skullduggery of any moment, within the contractor's ken, that he will be amenable to small deviations from the original drawings without smelling an excuse for an extra. He will not, from the opening gun, seek permission to substitute something that "is just as good," as some operators do (having banked on a series of these substitutions to offset the low figure they submitted to win the job). In fine, he's your best bet.

When a figure is submitted it is taken apart

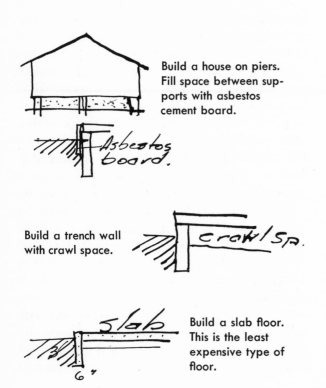

Use low ceiling heights, or ceilings low at one side.

by the architect. He asks who the subcontractors are, considers their general record for performance and questions a sub's bid that looks too low. He is not trying to make the house cost more, but if there is some special millwork included, perhaps a fancier staircase than ordinary, and the mill's figure is pretty clearly inadequate to do the job well enough, then it is best to know at once. Perhaps he should get another mill's figure for the work, or perhaps apprehension will be dispelled by discovery that the mill has a low overhead. It is a question of judgment, with the salient fact in mind that a naturally poor workman cannot do a good job no matter what he promises.

STICKS AND STONES

Build a house on piers. Fill space between supports with asbestos cement board.

Build a trench wall with crawl space.

Build a slab floor. This is the least expensive type of floor.

FOUNDATION MATERIALS vary according to locality, soil condition, building code or personal preference. Poured reinforced concrete is about ideal, being essentially waterproof and impervious to termites. Cement block on a poured concrete footing may be a little cheaper, but it should be in a dry location if there is to be a full or partial cellar. Sometimes the top course of block is filled solid with cement as a barrier against termites, but the always susceptible joints between blocks take away the guarantee.

Local conditions sometimes bring stone foundations into the picture on a competitive cost basis but they become increasingly rare, and less necessary because the top of the foundation wall seldom or never shows above ground.

Where there is no cellar, and the district code permits, the house may be set on concrete posts and grade beams, a not very common expedient

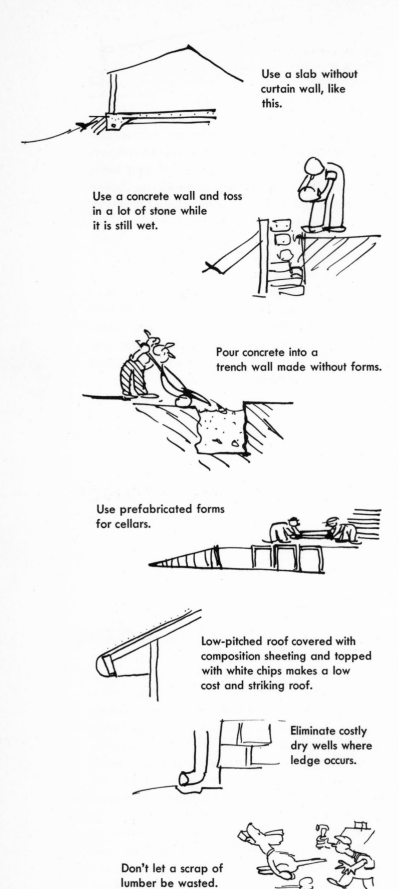

Use a slab without curtain wall, like this.

Use a concrete wall and toss in a lot of stone while it is still wet.

Pour concrete into a trench wall made without forms.

Use prefabricated forms for cellars.

Low-pitched roof covered with composition sheeting and topped with white chips makes a low cost and striking roof.

Eliminate costly dry wells where ledge occurs.

Don't let a scrap of lumber be wasted.

which avoids digging trenches below frost for a continuous wall, and is supposed to save money. It may on occasion.

The slab on ground, with perimeter resting on a concrete block wall that goes below frost, is now very common for radiant heated floors in cellarless houses. A large number of the resilient flooring materials are unsuited for use in this situation, though the non-resilient (brick, stone, tile) are available if desired. If you have strong opinions on flooring it might even rule out the slab-on-ground.

For all ordinary purposes there are two types of construction, wood and masonry. Poured concrete is rarely used for houses in the Northeast and patented systems, usually involving light metal construction, have not yet found wide acceptance. Their individual merit is a matter for study, as is their comparative cost.

Wood side walls do not leak, but masonry is less impervious. An eight inch brick wall cannot be depended upon in this regard as well as brick veneer, which is only four inches thick but has wood sheathed with waterproofed building paper behind it and pencil rods at the bottom to let the water out. Water gets through at the joints unless they are well and honestly laid and the mortar composition has a proper amount of lime. This is especially true of block construction, which also has a tendency to crack in a manner less harmful than unsightly, though this may be generally avoided by horizontal re-inforcing about every third course. There are many variations on the masonry theme but suffice it to give these few main points.

Wood walls in themselves are warmer than masonry walls but each may be bettered through insulating, with the wood still ahead.

One cannot make a hard and fast cost analysis between wood and masonry owing to diverse types and local conditions, but a rough differential of ten per cent above wood construction may be fairly near in the case of brick veneer.

For the extra expense in veneer the only practical gain is a fire resistant exterior that does not need painting. With solid masonry you have a wall that is fireproof and permanent, without appreciable maintenance costs. In neither case have you dodged painting expense entirely, because wood trim in cornices and around windows must be preserved and it is the more fussy type of work.

With so much in favor of wood be it said that attempts have been made to produce sidewall coverings that do not need periodic painting, but get along very nicely on less expensive stain or oil. There are even asphalt and asbestos sidings, but they raise the issue of esthetics. How far will you go to avoid upkeep expense; not too far one hopes.

The selection of roofing has all the familiar controls and maybe a few more. Beyond a degree of flatness (about thirty per cent) shingles cannot be used, and where they are used wood shingles are ruled out in some building codes. This is somewhat of a blow because they have a superior texture that cannot be duplicated in other materials with equal economy. Their effective life is at least as long as the asphalt strip shingles you are forced to use as a budget alternate. The more costly asbestos shingles and slate are good looking, fireproof and quite permanent.

Low pitches require metal, roll roofing or tar and gravel. Asphalt roll roofing is about as inexpensive as any you will find and is suitable for all pitches from steep to flat. It has no serious practical disadvantage, merely the esthetic handicap of no character and a long association with shacks and outbuildings.

Metal roofing is about the only solution for small flat or low pitched surfaces, where it is usually copper. That metal has graced many a roof and belfry tower and the characteristic green of its patina is a familiar sight. In housework where, for some reason metal is chosen as a roofing material, probably because of low pitch, the less expensive metals are used, such as non-ferrous aluminum, or "galvanized iron" which must be kept painted.

Tar and gravel is the standard for flat or almost flat roofs. Built up with alternate layers of roofing felt and pitch, mopped on, its durability is excellent and when constructed by some companies carries with it a guarantee for a period of years.

The visual test for a roof is a pleasing texture and color, though the latter is a point for great discretion. On the pitched roofs where this test applies wood, asbestos and slate are best by all odds and in that order. The practical test, without budgeting, would still select those materials; with budgeting and the wood tabu of building codes you find yourself using asphalt shingles and trying to like them.

SOUND ADVICE AND THE MULTIPURPOSE ROOM

As MORE THINGS HAPPEN in the living room than one could shake a stick at it is the proper place to start our examination, and an assumption based on averages would run about like this.

During the week, except as a small child's play area, it is practically unused in the morning and early afternoon, barring a meeting of the Ladies' Aid. By late afternoon the infant, if any, has been transferred to his or her nursery and older children may drift in from play or school. After dinner and dishwashing the whole family, exclusive of the minor infantry, foregathers in the living room at least temporarily. For the parents it is perhaps a routine evening of reading and small conversation. For the children there is homework and these two general items are not incompatible.

But of course our "normal" condition is riven with deviations and, unfortunately for easy planning the tyranny of sound, either as home produced music or from TV or radio speakers, immediately creates a situation unfavorable to the pursuits of some, forces attention or makes concentration on other matters a redoubtable feat of will. Someone has to get out or be frustrated and we may assume that, although the parents have a superior option on occupying the living room, circumstances always alter cases.

In houses with children acting as individuals, as they have a habit of doing, it is an unsafe supposition that mutually incompatible living room activities will be so staggered in timing that they may be successfully planned for in one room. Either it majors in quietude or, as is usually the case, it features sonic disturbances that do not support the cultivation of thought or major improvement of the mind. This seems to preclude such a dual use of the living room and calls for a quiet area in study or bedroom,

The front and back parlors of the past were useful for segregating functions, perhaps incompatible for simultaneous observance in one

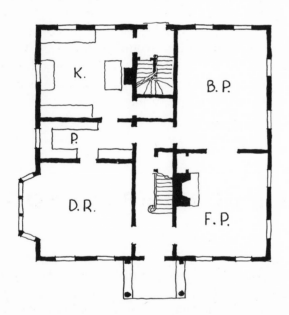

Front and back parlors of the pre-living room era.

room. Some of us, in old houses, still have them, with the back parlor presently masquerading as a study. House designers have not labelled any areas as such for three or four decades.

The study is a genuinely multipurpose room

for quiet activities, but has been known to double in brass if need be. For apart from its daily service to the thinking man and child it may be used as an emergency guest room or, when illness suggests isolating the patient, as a very conveniently located sick room. In families with adolescent children and their social evenings at home a study makes an easy retreat for parents, until such time as the age-group advances towards usurpation of the whole living area, plus kitchen, and forces a parental flight to the bedroom.

The bedroom has great potentialities as a dual-purpose room if it is more than a cubicle for sleeping. Among children it is not recommended for unsupervised play in groups, but the rightful child occupant may keep himself interested in toys, hobby or radio for hours on end. Here he may enjoy all the horrors of the airwaves without inflicting them on his more discriminating elders.

For adults the bedroom is readily expanded to meet the activities outlined above. Although for decades it was limited to bed, washstand and bureau, with a chair or two, there was the laggard discovery that a reading table or a writing desk could be equally useful. This in the capacity of refuge for parents, as a living room for the aged.

The excavation of a full basement has ceased to be inevitable these several years. Its partial demise is probably due to two or three things. Initially the modernist architect found no place for it in his credo. His exaltation of unlimited glass found the average unlighted cellar abhorrent to every right thinking person. Then there was the much increased ground coverage of the one story house, which really made full excavation inadvisable. Finally, increasing costs seemed to argue against unnecessary excavation.

The corollary to this omission is that you have to keep your possessions above ground in more expensive storage or deny yourself the ownership of as much gear. And along with the departed storage there is the vanishing game room. No one ever argued that this partially underground room had an ideal location, but it was relatively cheap space, and as an area for the more robustious games and social events it was a blessing to the refugees no less than to the participants. Few small house budgets can be stretched to include such a room above ground, so the living room has to bear the brunt.

If your family is a "going concern" you come equipped with furniture; if it is still in evolution there will be more to buy. Enough, say, to make life supportable for all your family at once, with even a guest or two on hand. The arranging of this paraphernalia then becomes the architect's problem, under your personal reviewing.

The living room must house the gear and at the same time permit grouping the elements of such varied activities as gatherings before the fireplace or about the piano, a spot or two for reading and a secondary center for conversation or games. The controls that suggest locations are planned features such as fireplace, windows, bookcases and the placement of your more important furniture. All these must be considered as vital points in the planning process, and as the room takes preliminary shape a set of cardboard cutouts of your furniture, to scale, will be a great help in making arrangements to insure the final workability of the room.

The environs of the fireplace have the most valuable square footage and are the heaviest taxed, in season and out. A davenport and two or more comfortable chairs, plus an end table and a coffee table are suggested. They may be grouped, roughly, about the fireplace sitters' half circle, with the clear implication that that area is a gathering place, not a thoroughfare.

Sometimes a davenport before the fireplace is backed by a table and the two lend their services to general reading, but probably not too well from the point of view of natural light and the risk of interference with conversationalists. A window has first claim to the title of reading center. A secondary reading center, perhaps no more than an easy chair, light and ash tray stand, will be convenient for evening use.

The piano has no competing demands with other departments except in the matter of

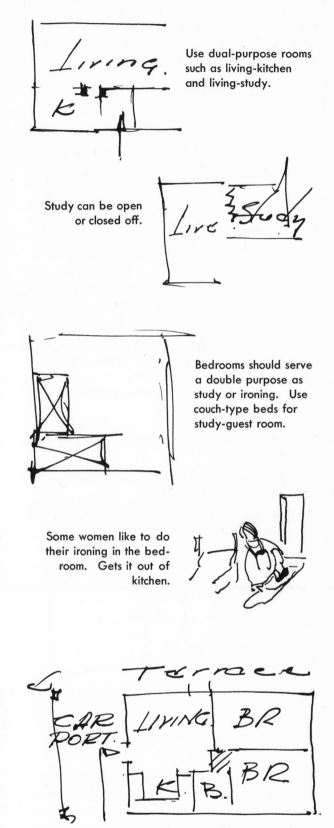

Use dual-purpose rooms such as living-kitchen and living-study.

Study can be open or closed off.

Bedrooms should serve a double purpose as study or ironing. Use couch-type beds for study-guest room.

Some women like to do their ironing in the bedroom. Gets it out of kitchen.

Cut hall space to absolute minimum while still maintaining good circulation.

chairs. Certainly the bench is solely a musical adjunct, but an extra straight chair or two nearby serve an occasionally useful purpose and may be borrowed.

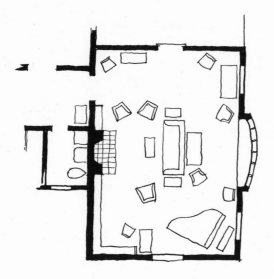

A living room furniture arrangement.

Other potential centers are influenced by TV or radio sets, bookshelving and games played on tables.

The usual warning may be sounded against the error of letting your living room become a common passageway, to the injury of its proper functions. Direct access to the outside may be a space-saver, because it means you have no entrance hall. But it is no boon to the living room, especially in winter, when you not only share your privacy with every one who rings the door bell, but are given a generous extra

dividend of frigid air. A direct access door to a garden terrace or living porch is quite another matter, for it is normally closed from fall to spring.

The fireplace needs no defense but its setting calls for thought. In small house design there is a very good chance that doors and windows will tend to crowd in upon it, and either tends to hurt its forefront as a gathering place. The door is an obvious threat because it suggests a thoroughfare. As to the window, the classic tradition of the fireplace envisaged a mighty chimney, from whose splayed recesses was radiated heat for cooking and bodily comfort. Though paneling may have covered the masonry you had a feeling of its hidden mass, and it was a reassuring thought seven months out of twelve. Its generous bulk where it emerged through the roof was the characteristic of a well appointed house. Even now, when all we really need is a spindling chimney above roof, we regularly build it over-size to avoid an appearance of meanness, so strong is the inherited tradition thereon. In old houses there never could be windows close by a great chimney, though of course it was seldom on an outside wall anyway, in the beginning, and even now they do not look right nearby it. Furthermore, the fireplace wall is not usually a brightly lighted surface, the fire sufficing for both radiation and soft illumination. A narrowly flanking window intrudes a light source during the day, in particular, that robs the fireplace of its focal rights, does no one any good and commits an esthetic offense.

COME INTO THE KITCHEN

THE FIRST AMERICAN KITCHENS, in farms and minor houses, were the principal rooms; the warmest and the pleasantest spot under a roof. If one is lucky enough to have experienced even a few summers of farm life, before the push-

button era brought its complications, he will have had a first-hand experience of simple living; of rocking chairs, of the small metal tub that was dragged out on bathing nights, of shaving before a little mirror that was propped on the meeting rail of a window over the sink, a window that framed Old Speck and Goose Eye to westward, of the bustling farm wife and the savors of her ample cookery.

The late nineteenth century kitchen was just gloomy and uninspired, by any judgment; it must have looked formidable even to the Victorian eye. Rather later, when the profitable market for ingenuity and better equipment began to come in as one's domestic bowed out, there developed a great furore for efficient, white kitchens, that conserved the energy, possibly for less important matters, and were altogether characterless and uninteresting.

We are still conserving energy, through the joint effort of architectural thought and manufacturing techniques, but we have learned a great deal about a kitchen's broad usefulness, and how it may be made pleasant as well as aseptic. Where there is imagination and a little more money than the indispensible minimum, one often finds that the lingering inspiration of the farm kitchen has returned to gladden our hearts. A more ample room than in recent years, the modern version has warmth in its use of wood for sheathing and cabinets, in its bricked fireplace, and space for sitting and eating. As an operating unit, replete with storage and mechanical gear it may assume a shape in plan that is not purely "L," "U" or "in line," the three classic kitchen layouts. But this is of no great moment unless the housewife has preternaturally weak feet and must save every step she can.

Although it is an intellectual delight to rationalize systems of design and make "flow-diagrams" to show how one surpasses another in step-saving (a step here, a motion there), it is reasonably certain that the normal housewife is not working on as narrow a factor of physical strength as has been alleged, nor is her perception acute enough to detect the theoretical betterment of many a slight plan adjustment, however much it may delight the planner.

To be free of these restrictive beliefs often permits one to design a handsome, more generally useful room, but one which is still efficient in its important relationships between work centers.

A basic flow-diagram of kitchen planning sets

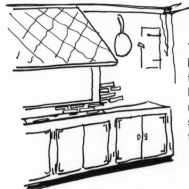

The living-kitchen has brought back the roomy old-type kitchens of our grandmothers. Built-in stoves take away the clinical look.

Use open shelves in the kitchen if your equipment is decorative.

With kitchens and living rooms now practically one, some screening is necessary to shut out the clutter. This simple screen and pass-through is the answer.

A bamboo screen can be used to shut off work area of kitchen. Relatively inexpensive.

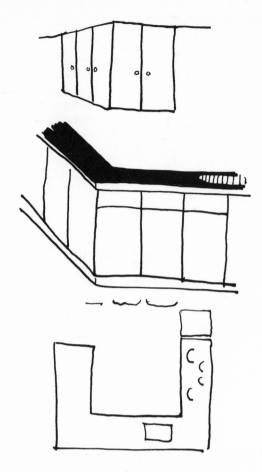

A kitchen planned in this way has the advantage of one entrance with overhead cupboards and base cabinets open from both sides.

Lights can be recessed in underside of upper cabinets; will light up stove.

up six steps—
  (a) The delivery of food.
  (b) Food storage.
  (c) Food preparation.
  (d) Cooking.
  (e) Serving.
  (f) Restoring order.

Obviously it's convenient to have one's refrigerator near the service entrance, but who is going to have a nervous breakdown if it is five feet (two steps) away? It is far more important to have a counter by the refrigerator for placing food during transfer.

The vital disciplines in kitchen design concern the interrelationship between preparation, cooking and cleaning. Traditionally the sink is flanked by two work counters, at the end of one being the refrigerator, at the other end the range. The last named may be near the dining area, but, if the plan makes that difficult, two or three steps further should not give great concern except to the theoretician.

If this three-point nerve center is not in a straight line, but is bent to an "L," it obviously reduces steps between extremes, if given yet another bend, into a "U," all points are equidistant from the kitchen's center.

The complete function of the kitchen in any given house plan will control design—

(a) In the home with servants it may be solely a work center, separated from a formal dining room by a pantry.

(b) Its first simplification may have it open directly into a dining room or "alcove," and have a "breakfast nook" or "snack bar" within its confines, as well as a restricted office space for cookbooks, files, writing.

(c) The next step is to combine the kitchen and all the eating area in a large, fireplaced room, pleasantly reminiscent of the farm kitchen but vastly more efficient per ounce of energy expended.

(d) Finally, in the open plan, the kitchen is separated from other living areas on one or two sides only by its working counter.

From its nineteenth century relegation to limbo the kitchen reassumes its status as the most useful and best loved room in the house. In detail it goes thoroughly mechanical on refrigeration, dishwashing, garbage disposal and cooking. The first three services have made an orderly progress in improved design, and so has cooking, but with a few growing pains.

When the march of "progress" discarded the old high oven stove and fell for indiscriminate "streamlining," we found ourselves in receipt of too low ovens and even lower broilers. Many the housewife who hated to confess that her early fascination for the sleek, white beauties was later tempered by the unpleasant bending exercises attendant upon baking and broiling. Came the dawn when an intelligent manufacturer decided that the range wasn't going anywhere to require streamlining and that its component parts didn't need to be in one package anyway. So we made substantial progress and may now place the cooking top where it comes best in our counter, and locate the oven beside it or build it into the kitchen casework anywhere and at whatever height is desired. There may be two ovens, or special grilles and barbecues, as the taste and pocketbook decide.

Next after the machinery it would seem that counter tops receive enough wear and tear to make the owner conscious of their importance.

(a) Stainless steel is immensely durable, easily maintained and expensive. Perhaps it might be restricted to the sink.

(b) Linoleum is very commonly used because it is cheaper and colorful, but it must be laid right to resist water, will not tolerate cutting edges and has to be waxed to avert water spots.

(c) Plastic tops come in many colors and they are more impervious to stains, burns and scratches than linoleum, more expensive as well.

(d) Wood tops, unfortunately, haven't been fashionable in recent years. No one advertises wood tops for sale, so they never will become modish, which is really too bad. If a good hard wood is used (once it was cherry) it will outwear the owner, is easy to keep clean, makes an excellent cutting surface and has a lovely warm tone to harmonize with the friendly, but not the "aseptic" kitchen. In almost all kitchens there is at least a wood counter section for carving, tacit admission that the material is good, if not chi-chi.

Wall cabinets have become more economical in enameled steel, than in wood, which settles the matter for most people. However, for converts to the family-type kitchen there is usually no hesitation about selecting wood.

All cabinet doors come solid or glazed, as you wish, and some shelving may properly be left open, an obvious case being the often used spice and condiment shelf.

As to wall surfacing—

(a) The family kitchen is likely to use wood, filled, lacquered and waxed. It may be pine sheathing, hardwood or plywood.

Don't smother from smoke. Use a kitchen range hood.

Hood over cooking gives character and serves to take off spit smoke and odors.

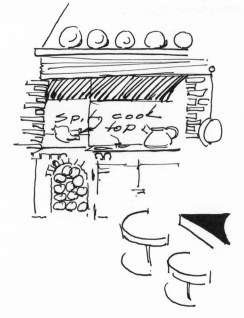

(b) Plastic coated wall paper or fabric is a worthy favorite. It is a boon for restorers because it covers cracks in existing plaster, and always it's easily cleaned with a damp cloth.

(c) Paint has ever been the popular covering and here again plastic paints have reputed virtues of durability.

(d) Tile coverings are several in number—

1) Ceramic, which is impervious to everything but the sledge hammer and washes as easily as one might expect. Useful about sinks and ranges, expensive but very long wearing.

2) Color-glazed metal tiles (in sheets), able to withstand all normal abuse and most thoughtlessness; much cheaper than ceramic, but not free.

3) Aluminum and stainless steel "tiling," tough, fire-resistant, grease-proof.

4) Plastic tiles in colors. Also grease-proof and easily cleaned with soap and water. Not easily stained, less durable than tiles 1 and 3, but adequately long-lived.

Even the "family-kitchen" enthusiast reneges on using a wooden floor, which would be quite supportable and longer lasting than some others, but is harder to maintain. Among the common types—

(a) Linoleum leads all others. But it has got to be laid right if it is to remain supine and wear evenly. The underfloor may well be plywood sheets, or magnesite (which, being a plastic material, initially, is ideal for producing a smooth surface in alteration work). Linoleum is available in the familiar sheets, or as tile which may be replaced where necessary. It is grease resistant and its life is greatly prolonged by waxing.

(b) Plastic flooring, that comes in the same two forms as linoleum, sheet or tile, is a newer rival. It claims all of the latter's virtues as well as a sturdy disregard for abrasion and the optional use of wax.

To win its way, despite advertising, any new material must give as much for less money, or a lot more for a little extra investment. There are many of them and they enter the market without proper certification of the manufacturer's claims. Actual experience by numerous people and through enough time and under varied circumstances, alone gives a true answer. The flash of novelty and "up-to-date-ism" should not be recognized as valid reasons for spending a client's money.

(c) Vinyl cork, a plastic over cork, is reputedly excellent. The plastic covering is immune to stains and clinging dirt, while the cork gives a quiet resilience. More costly than (a) or (b), as much as rubber tile, it has not had the latter's thorough testing, and the bond between plastic and cork is not necessarily above suspicion.

(d) Rubber tile is a fine material for the

Another hooded barbecue —

Most kitchen barbecues are raised on a high shelf for convenience.

kitchen floor; not cheap (though what is?), but good for years of service, resisting stain, friendly to panel heat and easily cleaned.

(e) Asphalt tile, the least expensive of resilient floorings, comes in a grease-resistant form and is amenable to panel heating. There is a fine variety of colors, but all asphalt tile requires the same waxing maintenance as linoleum.

(f) Hard-burned brick is sometimes used for "family- type" kitchens, where the structural floor is an on-the-ground concrete slab. It is expensive and is not resilient but has virtues, not the least being its unending ability to withstand wear, the hardest kind of wear. A completely fireproof floor, it is impervious, easily cleaned, and an important feature of the room's esthetic coloring.

(g) Quarry tile makes a beautiful, costly floor, having all the virtues of good clay tile, charm of color and a completely impervious surface.

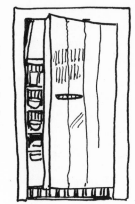

A built-in refrigerator with a stainless steel front. Works in well with compartmented stoves in living-kitchens.

A 3-compartment refrigerator opens both sides into kitchen and dining space. Believe it or not, it hangs from the ceiling. Gets that bulky affair off the floor.

DINING AS OF TODAY

MOST VULNERABLE OF AREAS for extinction, under pressure from several quarters, the dining room has almost come to have an honorific status like a vast lawn that implies wealth for its maintenance or a platinum bath tub, though it is as useful as ever in a menage that retains a trace of old fashioned formality.

The reasons for this decline are obvious, apart from the housewife's disinclination to maintain a ritual that makes extra work for her, in an era which has lost its appreciation of form. Used only two hours a day, taking 160 or more square feet, at a variable (but always rising) cost per foot, the dining room as a one-purpose area begins to look like an extravagance to the average client.

An early mass-move in contemporary plan-

ning, dating from the depressed thirties and manifested in the famous General Electric house design competition, overwhelmingly demoted the dining room to a dining area. Lucky for it that we all have to eat or it would have been given short shrift instead of a corner of the living room. This competition had a powerful effect in crystallizing a tendency that had been developing for several years, and since then some avant-garde design has been known to relegate the eating process to stools along a counter, which seems to approach the final degradation, even though the kitchen and living room are opened to one another.

The fact that the multipurpose living room is the dominating area, that it can hardly be made big enough, under cost restrictions, and

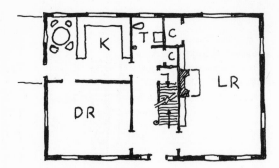

Typical dining room before devolution began.

quality of the room. About all you can hope for is a room for eating completely apart from the living area which, between times, may serve as a second living room, study, music room (with no piano), or auxiliary office. There will have to be extensive storage facilities to simplify the

that its use is never simultaneous with a dining room's cuts the props from under the latter.

If you want an isolated dining room, under a limited budget, and many people do, there is a possibility that it, too, may be made multipurpose, though at some sacrifice to the original

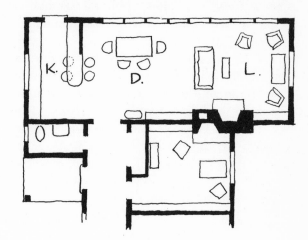

2d phase — living-dining-kitchen in one room.

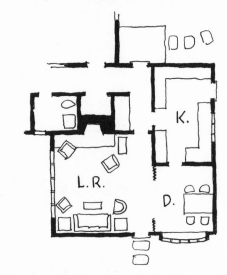

Vanishing dining room. 1st phase — as alcove of living room.

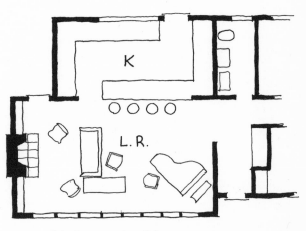

3d phase — the dining room gone; a living room-kitchen.

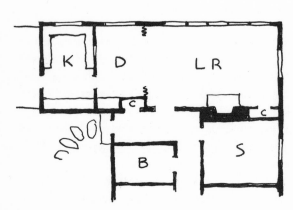

1st phase — at end of living room.

tidying up between uses and the sideboard and china cupboard's old duties fall to the lot of a storage wall between dining and food preparation.

If the privilege of screening the dining area before and after eating is your main requirement consider a folding partition or a drapery, with dining in an ell or an alcove off the living room. This is far better than the indignity of sitting on bar stools though somewhat short of

28

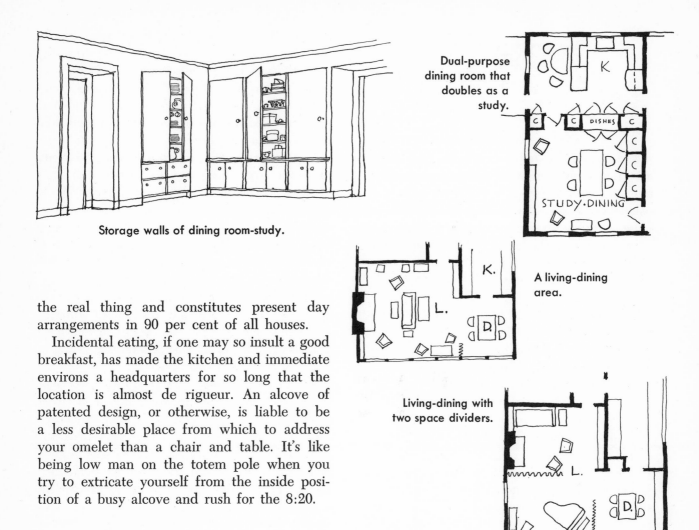

Storage walls of dining room-study.

Dual-purpose dining room that doubles as a study.

A living-dining area.

Living-dining with two space dividers.

the real thing and constitutes present day arrangements in 90 per cent of all houses.

Incidental eating, if one may so insult a good breakfast, has made the kitchen and immediate environs a headquarters for so long that the location is almost de rigueur. An alcove of patented design, or otherwise, is liable to be a less desirable place from which to address your omelet than a chair and table. It's like being low man on the totem pole when you try to extricate yourself from the inside position of a busy alcove and rush for the 8:20.

THE MATTER OF SLEEPING

IT IS NOT ASKING TOO MUCH that everyone should have a corner of his own to which he can escape, or retire to in dignified manner, for peace, isolation and sleep. Except in substandard housing this has been a widely observed rule, but there has not been much progressive thinking towards the bedroom's greater usefulness until recent years. But no unanimity of opinion is likely to be achieved, however long the problem is meditated.

To begin with there is the scientific approach regarding ideal conditions for sleep, which emphasize utter silence, complete darkness and carefully regulated heat and humidity. These considerations would so constrict the room's general usefulness, that any healthy person might well prefer to "bull-it-through" under familiar though less than perfect conditions.

There is the argument for a subdivision of the bedroom into a modest sleeping cubicle and an adjacent dressing room. Whereas the dressing room is excellent and useful equipment in houses that can stand the strain, there is almost always a generous bedroom. The sleep-

29

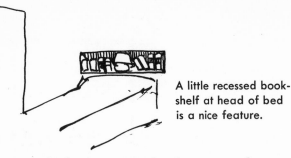

A little recessed book-shelf at head of bed is a nice feature.

ing cubicle is no popular favorite and except for invalids and cranky sleepers the complications of sound-absorbent surface materials, dark colors, mechanical ventilation and what not seem liberally over-rationalized. A secondary item that it permits (possibly) misguided fresh air sleeping without chilling the dressing room certainly has point, if you happen to indulge in that habit.

The next attempt at improvement concedes the defeat of the cubicle and seeks to organize the "old-fashioned" bedroom, that it may return you more for your money. Mind you, there is always a place for the "unimproved" bedroom, but if you are a little crowded there is much to be said for considering new devices.

Basic equipment is all too obvious and familiar, but we may refer to a few desirable features. First off the bed, or beds, should be so located that they may catch a cross draft in summer. You may occupy one of them eight hours a day, but except for the ventilation feature their location is less important than that of the other furniture, which enjoys at least occasional use the other sixteen hours. It is good if beds do not divide the room like promontories that have forever to be skirted, but that is not always easy. Upon entering one should have a straight route to the dresser, clothes storage, dressing room or bath room without your four-poster's interposition. Dresser, toilet table, chaise longue, chairs and benches will be to personal preference, but something to remember is a well lighted, full length mirror,

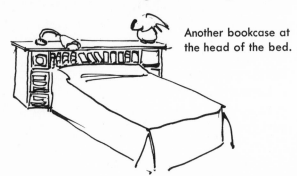

Another bookcase at the head of the bed.

and an adequate amount of free floor area before it.

In addition to traditional equipment there are other pieces suggested by the bedroom's secondary use, as a sitting room or study. We have touched on this under *Sound Advice and the Multipurpose Room.*

Especially in the modern house, with its wide-open plan, there is a sharp decline in one's chances to enjoy a degree of privacy. It is hardly the terrible experience of living in a crowded barracks, but more than one modern house owner has come to feel a twinge of pity every time he passes a bowl of goldfish. Even though he is gregarious to a fault there are moments when he would relish having fewer people about or somewhat less infantile tumult, a common reaction in moments of mental concentration. If you haven't a study, consider a table or desk in a bedroom.

A thoroughgoing multipurpose bedroom might call for a disappearing door-bed, or a so-called Hollywood bed skulking in a corner (to give the maximum useful free area for other furniture), a storage wall or extra closet space to take the materials for its secondary usage. These could be drawing or sketching gear, household records, garden or church club records, wildflower herbarium, sewing materials, toys, a boy's collection of almost anything, books for the student.

The usual house has at least three bedrooms, as dictated by average family size and sexes. The owner's or master's bedroom prefers its own bath, but because it also has to be near the nursery bedroom the two rooms sometimes connect to the same bath, which is not ideal when the child grows older. If the layout is ample enough a small nursery may lead directly to the master's bedroom, for future conversion to some other purpose, such as a dressing room or sewing room. Considering the always possible event of illness there is something to be said for bedrooms en suite, even without a bath between them. Although it might be idyllic to have a master's bedroom well isolated from the others a mother knows that she is on round-the-clock call where there are children and it is therefore convenient to be in a central location.

THE ORDER OF THE BATH

A water closet in a separate enclosure gives greater use to one bath.

Tuck in an extra lavatory with w.c. backed up to bath.

This makes a good dual bath but extra door needed for privacy costs almost as much as extra toilet.

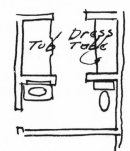

That extra bath can be squeezed in with an enameled iron corner shower.

A prefabricated enameled iron shower saves tile or plaster and studding.

Here's a good idea for a duo bath with shower between.

Double baths are best but you can put an extra lavatory in bedroom backed up to bath with curtain or wood cupboard-door.

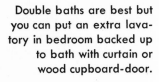

WE MAY HAVE A NATIONAL PENCHANT for painting the lily—we certainly have for spending money, or perhaps it's just a meritorious urge to invest our mechanical props with beauty—but the bathroom has come a long way since its components were first gathered in one room.

Antedating that happy event the three basic parts were in separate locations, primitive but flexible, and seemed to answer every current demand. The advent of plumbing changed this fine dispersal of our conveniences, put them in one room and, among most families, tied up the use of any two while one person used the third. We countered by duplicating the services when there was money enough, and by instituting the first floor powder room.

Came the inflationary spiral of post-war years and, though some said, "We never had it so good," it wasn't good enough to keep up with the rising cost of building. The extra bathrooms had to be dropped or curtailed, and even the powder room had to undergo a consideration of pros and cons. Once again the dawdlers were in a fair way to cause traffic jams during a bathroom's rush hours.

The compartmented bath is our best answer to such a dilemma, for it has the tub or shower, and the watercloset in separate cubicles, the lavatory in one or both of them. Thus, in a one-story house the powder room may be the watercloset and lavatory of a, or the, bathroom, accessible from a corridor, while the adjacent tub unit may open to a bedroom or to the same corridor. The possible variations are endless and inside units quite feasible with skylights or clerestory windows.

Improved planning has enabled us to wring more use out of each unit, and that is in good part due to storage facilities. When fixture man-

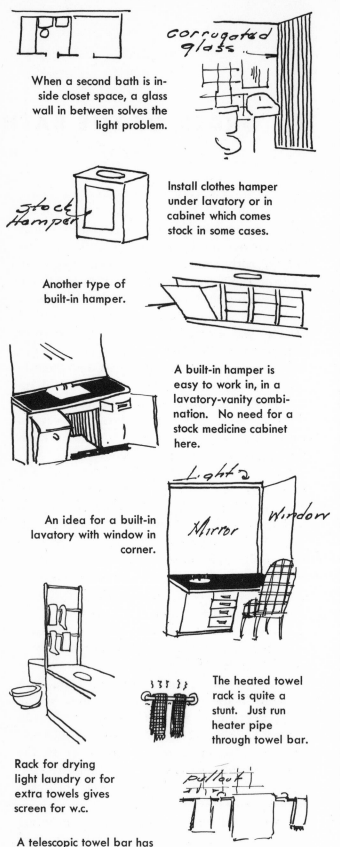

When a second bath is inside closet space, a glass wall in between solves the light problem.

corrugated glass

Install clothes hamper under lavatory or in cabinet which comes stock in some cases.

stock Hamper

Another type of built-in hamper.

A built-in hamper is easy to work in, in a lavatory-vanity combination. No need for a stock medicine cabinet here.

An idea for a built-in lavatory with window in corner.

Light *Mirror* *Window*

The heated towel rack is quite a stunt. Just run heater pipe through towel bar.

Rack for drying light laundry or for extra towels gives screen for w.c.

pullout

A telescopic towel bar has ends that pull out for extra hanging space.

ufacturers sought to exalt the beauty (and cost) of their lavatories by disengaging them from the marble or wood in which they had been set we went along with the gag and never realized until too late that we had lost our valuable counter space. It took a number of years before the elegance of the new trend wore thin and we turned back to bowls set in counters. Again there was space for the temporary placing of toilet gear and clothes. An extension of the counter, perhaps as dressing table, and good organization for storage of the space thereunder, made a genuine betterment. These features are available in ready-made units, in a variety of combinations, both wall-hung and set upon the floor. In some, a pull-out step in front of the lavatory makes it easier for a small child. True enough, the minimum watercloset-lavatory cubicle will have very little space for a counter-set bowl, but it is the exception where no improvement is possible. In the case of a small bathroom a counter height storage wall may sometimes be built at the foot of an otherwise "corner" tub. Even so small a top makes a most useful counter.

The storage wall with shelving, along one side of a bathroom, fronted with sliding mirrors, gives one more space than he could possibly wish for and takes towels, medicines, "sundries" galore. Sometimes a plan permits a more orthodox closet to the same effect, plus a medicine cabinet. If you have two of the latter keep one locked and your children out of trouble, or lock your single cabinet and have a smaller one to take toothbrushes, soap, drinking glass, etc. Don't skimp on towel bars; one might even have a heated bar for bath towels, where forced hot water is available. There ought to be a chair or stool, and of course there must be if a dressing table is included in a master's bath. Bath exhaust fans, located as high up as is convenient, are useful for removing damp, steamy air, and in the case of a bath-dressing room combination the fan is more important. Here the intervening door is seldom closed and adjacent clothes storage may not be improved by the steaming.

The bathroom layout administers to family convenience and is simultaneously subject to plumbing costs that often clash and force a balance to be struck between desire and budget. Though the one-story house is freed from economical first and second floor plumbing relationships, there are clear economies if piping is concentrated; kitchen adjacent to the bathroom or two bathrooms back to back. The very simplest layout of all would be three inline bathroom fixtures, backed up against the kitchen-laundry, with no other water outlets but the hose bibbs. Clearly these restrictive facts affect planning and give the higher-budget house a freedom that should be turned to good account throughout its design.

We have been speaking of the workaday, compartmented bathroom, but it has three or four more complex relatives, all of which fit easily into the one story house.

Take the combination bath-laundry, and this connotes the use of mechanical laundry equipment, washer, ironer, dryer. The argument is that there is no more vital relation between modern laundry gear and any one area of the house, than between it and the main source of its reason for being, cloth to be washed that originates in bed, bath and dressing rooms. A literal interpretation with all fixtures in one room has an obviously limited practicality; better the two services back to back, with a partition between.

Another variant is the bath and scrub-up combination. This latter feature used to be handled in two story houses with cellars, by a basement shower and toilet. Gardeners and players, coming in from their exertions, divested themselves of their earth-begrimed or perspiry togs and bathed before going up into the house. In one-story, often basementless houses the scrub-up shower or foot bath comes naturally as an adjunct to a main floor bathroom. In more elaborate layouts it may be an independent unit immediately accessible to the out of doors, and then its full use as a mud-room is permissible, without being an offense to the true bath's cleanliness. Still another variant is the isolated, three-fixtured layout, placed near work area or swimming pool.

After the decline and fall of the Roman Empire it took some doing and innumerable

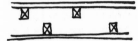
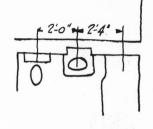

Line all fixtures on one wall.

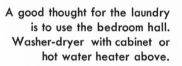

Allow for 2 separate walls on either side of plumbing pipes — makes for less cutting and fussing. Also less noise. Easy to soundproof.

Centralize bath and kitchen, or two baths and kitchen.

A good thought for the laundry is to use the bedroom hall. Washer-dryer with cabinet or hot water heater above.

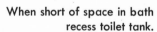

An extra water closet in the basement is a cheap substitute for a lavatory. Easy for kids to use.

When short of space in bath recess toilet tank.

A sliding plastic enclosure makes a luxury bath when compared to stock curtain.

Bathrooms need to lose that clinical look. Put the w.c. in a separate stall and have a little garden outside the window.

An after-note on the above. The two lavatories ease the load.

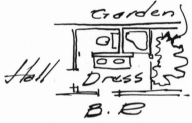

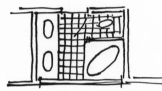

Two variations of the T-plan opening into a garden. One has tub — one has shower. Note two lavatories and recessed lights in the ceiling as well as ample storage space.

A combination heater and light in bath ceiling. Takes up no wall-space.

Use a fixed window in bath, plus a vent in ceiling. This gives an added feature at no extra cost.

years before bathing reacquired its status as being desirable, moral and pleasant. Which fetches us to the matter semi-*al fresco* bathing (in season, need one say). Here again the one-story house on a lot of reasonable size lends itself easily to what has been called the "garden bath." The outer bathroom wall is glazed to the floor and opens to the outside with a swing door or sliding glass panels. Of course the small garden beyond the portals is discreetly fenced or otherwise enclosed. All the fixtures are inside except a possible shower head for hot summer use. The liberal glazing of bathrooms is not uncommon, where they give onto remote or well landscaped areas, or look upon ground that slopes away.

The apotheosis of this arrangement, obtainable by anyone with a sturdy budget (in the heavyweight class and no glass jaw) is the foregathering of all these pleasant features, a small sheltered flower garden, sunbathing, the glass walled bathroom and a sunken bathing pool whose tilings are radiant heated. It is apparent that even modernity is not immune to liftings from the stuffy or ancient epochs, take the marble-topped counter of Victorian days, or the Roman bath with its heated floor.

Bathroom illumination is handled variously, with recessed fixtures, or by trough lighting. Shielded tube lights may line both sides of a mirror or the tubes may glow through obscure glass, which throws plenty of light on the person but isn't dazzling to obscure one's vision. Spotlights have their occasional use, and a low-wattage night light is desirable.

In many places the law requires bathroom light switches to be placed outside the entrance, as a safety measure against electric shock, when wet hands touch a faulty switch.

The simple minimum bathroom layout is 5' x 5', which functions, but is too small for comfort; 5' x 8' is better. The minimum water-closet lavatory cubicle is about 2' x 5', with an outswinging door. Whatever type of room is used, compartmented or otherwise, remember that it should be able to take two people at once, in the event of sickness.

Herewith a few "ifs" and "don'ts":

(A) Avoid windows over tubs, unless it's

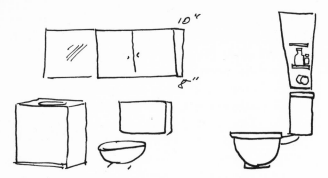

Section through
sloping cabinet
over seat.

This is a
good thought for
a clothes dryer
for the bath. A
toe-space radiator sends heat into cupboard to
dry clothes. Be sure and put in vent holes.

There's room over the seat for a big medicine
cabinet. It can slope out for extra storage.

double glazing and a fixed sash. The obvious reasons are unpleasant winter air cooling and the risk and difficulty of cleaning and operating.

(B) If you seriously object to the sound of water select as quiet a fixture as may be and insulate your bathroom, or have it shielded by closets.

(C) Don't forget that it is very convenient to have a shut-off for each faucet when washers are to be changed.

(D) If you use one-way glass in the lower half of your bathroom window be sure that it isn't turned wrong-side out.

(E) Don't forget that good piping is of first importance. Plumbing codes usually control essential sanitary details and proper venting, but there is latitude in water supply pipe sizes. Check with your architect on these points. Copper and brass piping is usually best and the chemical nature of the local water may restrict you to them. One hears amazing tales of pipe metal wasted by acid (soft) water, and clogged

pipes where the minerals of hard water are plated on until the flow is much reduced. Of course this difficulty requires a water softener, but in any event you and your architect must know the peculiarities of the supply you are going to use.

Bathroom flooring must face water and spilled medicines and should not be, but too often is, slippery. Kitchen floorings are equally suitable for the bathroom.

Counter tops in the bath, as in the kitchen, vary from ceramic tile to plastic laminates and linoleum, in many colors. They are subjected to about the same wear and tear (water, medicine, cigarette burns), but are spared the kitchen's cutting edges.

All of these materials have a color range that requires trained selection, preferably not by a salesman. There are no perfect solutions combining mayhem-proof surfaces at low cost. No matter what you come up with the children have got to be restrained from throwing iodine about.

Put pipes under bath to
warm it. These are just
the ordinary heat pipes.

Put a husky grab bar by tub,
set vertically. Should be
12″ to 15″ long, strongly
set to studs.

Use a tub with flanges
that go up under tile.

Here's a clever shower-
head that combines shower
and tub-filler. Good too
because of its adjustable
height for children.

WE ARE ALWAYS RIDING trends or fashions in all types of design, and most of them, except women's hats, are bolstered by seemingly indisputable arguments. Successive trends deny the loudly acclaimed validity of previous reasoning and furnish their own good theories on why the present fashion is a "must." It would occasion no cause for alarm if all changes displayed a general improvement. Unfortunately, they don't, and we have observed fortuitous swing-backs to earlier styles more than once.

This is by way of contrasting the present day mania for built-in storage with the split system of storing in movable furniture and closets. In our opinion there is much to be said on both sides.

In a few words the built-in is exactly designed storage, conveniently located and wonderful if you have anticipated your permanent demands correctly. If you haven't it begins to look vastly immovable and difficult of correction. Built-in installations in the living area are related to its varied uses, such as eating, reading, games, music making, etc. Now, whereas it is true that any given layout has a limited number of variations in the disposition of its parts, if it is to function properly, one has practically no opportunity to seek variety through minor change when tied to elaborate built-ins. There is no gainsaying the superior possibilities of nicely integrated built-in storage but it is not, *per se*, a cure-all; and sometimes seems to belie the contention that the one-story house has maximum flexibility. Finally, on the long view towards re-sale, your storage arrangements may look like built-in whimsy to a prospective buyer.

We have been speaking about visible installations which tie in with the similarly permanent construction of seats, table tops, desks, radio and TV cabinets to make a completely frozen layout for the living-dining area. We would not go so far as to condemn designed storage, as such, when it is isolated behind a wall surface. Even in that case there is still the later chance that you might want to shift the accent to more toy storage with less emphasis on the space for home movies, a much greater disposition towards records and sheet music and less for files and miscellany, but your living arrangement is not so hopelessly tied in with these changes of opinion.

Devices for storage are closets or storage walls, built-ins, movable furniture, attics and cellars. As the availability of the last two begins to vanish, with present building trends, the gear they once handled has to be given succor by the intermediate first floor. Both of these spaces are large storage areas and, despite their reputation for being a hodge-podge or dusty catch-alls, they do yeoman service for much necessary storage in excess of the junk they house. Furthermore they are relatively cheap. Admittedly the one-story house does not come easily by an attic, but the excavation of a partial cellar is mere child's play for a steamshovel. The alternative is a first floor utility room, smaller, lighter and much handier, but costing rather more per cubic foot of storage space.

Where no cellar is provided there's a good space under stairs which can be used for book storage.

The closet has a long record of inadequacy in design, volume and occurrence. How it could have been so neglected and left a source of perennial annoyance to the householder now escapes the imagination. Perhaps because of the little space it steals from the living area, perhaps because casework increases cost, perhaps through plain unimaginativeness.

Lately storage walls have helped absorb our goods and chattels. They may be counter height, under windows, or extend from floor to ceiling along corridors or between rooms. They may be rather shallow or a full two feet deep, depending on what they are to take. Characteristically they are fitted with a series of sliding or swing doors that open to reveal the shelving, pull-out trays, racks or hanging rods of typical present day storage. They are not cheap, being solid casework, and though potentially useful must be balanced against the budget.

Movable storage, besides the familiar chest, dresser, desk and wardrobe, may include modern pieces with good external pretensions as furniture and whose inward design is highly organized like a full-fledged built-in or storage wall. Yet they have the advantage of mobility for those who place a value on it.

For the purposes of our exposition let us assume a one-story house containing—

(a) Entrance and circulatory hall.
(b) Living-dining room.
(c) Kitchen-laundry with rear entry.
(d) Study.
(e) Master bedroom and bath.
(f) Two children's bedrooms and common bath.
(g) Utility room or cellar.
(h) Garage.

Within these areas we have to store hundreds of necessary and unnecessary objects, a discouraging list in its entirety, and as personal predilection will determine many devices and locations for tucking them away, let us take an average instance for description.

The entrance hall has the most positively located closet of all, for hats, scarves, overclothing and rain gear. With sliding panels or a pair of swing doors one may compartment the hanging rod and gum-shoe racks on one side,

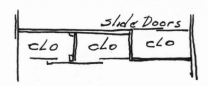

A 3-closet storage wall with sliding doors can be made out of pine or plywood.

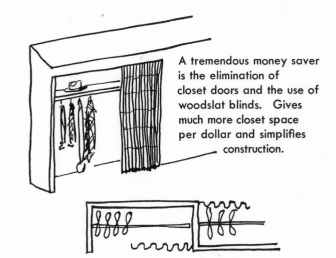

A tremendous money saver is the elimination of closet doors and the use of woodslat blinds. Gives much more closet space per dollar and simplifies construction.

Solid wood folding doors make wide openings for closets, save on trim wall, hardware, door, labor and painting.

Then there are similar basswood or bamboo doors. Closets using these are simply recesses — no trim, no jogs.

Use up all shallow spaces for closets. All closets need not be 2'-0" deep; 1'-0" will do rather than waste the space.

A bookcase and closet combination.

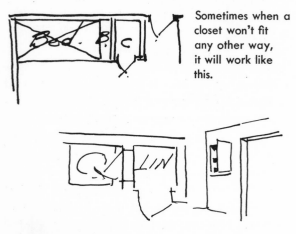

Sometimes when a closet won't fit any other way, it will work like this.

Door from bath to linen closet solves shortage of storage space in bath.

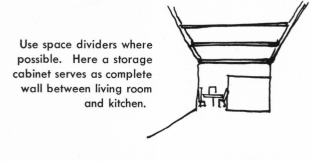

Use space dividers where possible. Here a storage cabinet serves as complete wall between living room and kitchen.

You can buy a tiny refrigerator which will fit in under a bookcase.

The answer to a low cost closet light. Switch snaps on when door is opened. It fastens to shelf. Only costs a dollar or two.

the hat shelves (or pegs) on the other, along with umbrella rack and shelving for scarves and gloves. For convenience it is imperative that nothing is piled, a satisfactory procedure for some closets but a misery for coat closets.

The ground coverage of the one-story house requires an augmented hallway for proper circulation, as we are fundamentally opposed to the less flexible arrangement of having to go through one room to reach another, of having to pass through a bedroom to reach a common toilet. Thus, the lengthened corridor, requiring no unbroken wall space for furniture placement, is susceptible to as much contiguous storage space as may be arranged. Here is absorbed the attic's old chore of storing such as out-of-season clothes, hand luggage, Christmas tree ornaments, camping equipment, old photographs, along with sheets, blankets, and possibly bath towels. It is optional for music, toys and games, small musical instruments, card tables and hobby gear. At the end farthest away from the kitchen there may be a broom and cleaning station. Sports equipment is sometimes split between hall storage and space in the utility room (or cellar), except the special case of firearms whose display often graces a study.

The living room, with its wall storage or built-ins may take radio, TV or a record player behind movable panels, and find quarters for a movie projector and collapsible screen, for records, sheet music, albums, scrapbooks, adult games and card tables. If there are bookshelves the under-counter space behind cupboard doors will help carry the load.

The nature of dining room or dining area storage is too obvious to itemize. The full-formed version may even have decorative china cupboards and a connecting pantry where there is bulk storage for china. Where the dining area is common with the kitchen, the kitchen casework usually encompasses all storage thereabout.

The problem of the kitchen-laundry is discussed elsewhere. Suffice it to say that they give onto the rear entry, which area may shoulder more responsibility than it used to. Now it may have a small toilet cubicle and a mud room for the children which, supplemented with a little family discipline, keeps much dirt and stain from the rest of the house.

A study stores the inevitable books, the files of written records, scrapbooks, albums, game material, a record player, decorative or valuable sports paraphernalia. With the study wall furred out for book shelving it is usually a simple matter to catch all of these things in adjacent casework. In either modern or traditional design it makes sense to start book shelving at counter height and have cupboard space below. There is never any dearth of material to fill such a space.

The design of the master bedroom depends on that useful adjunct, the dressing room or walk-through closet. In simpler form there is a minimum demand for two closets and ample furniture drawer space. One may make a storage wall in the bedroom and eliminate most of the furniture. Behind the slide or swinging doors will be shelving, shoe racks, hat trees, necktie bars, bag troughs, sliding trays for shirts, underwear, lingerie, collars, handkerchiefs, stockings, etc., and hanging rods. Be it storage wall or wall closet the minimum depth is 20″ for a hanging pole. Allow 2″ per garment along the pole, and do not have the closet extend over a foot beyond the limits of the door or doors. The pole is about 5′–6″ from the floor, except for evening gowns of truly regal length. Space above the pole works out simply as high shelving, but preferably it should be sealed off from the hanging area and have small cupboard doors of its own. Fitted closets come in prefabricated units, which may cut the cost of a fairly expensive detail.

With a dressing room or walk-through closet most of this complex of clothes storage moves out of the bedroom.

Secondary bedroom storage for children should be expansible for adolescence. Until such time the bottom of their closet might have low cupboards for infant toys, with shoe space above and plenty left over for hanging clothes. In the case of boys there can hardly be too many of these cupboarded storage alcoves (rather than a general catch-all closet) if a semblance of tidiness is to be maintained right up through high school days. Their collecting mania produces a discouraging clutter, even though it be only "comics."

In basementless houses, with heaters and hot water tanks hidden in closets or utility rooms the latter must be organized with shelves and racks for the storage of tools, screens, storm windows, bicycles, garden furniture, hose, and miscellaneous gardening equipment. A slightly oversized garage may take some of the pressure off the utility room, with work bench, a place for the baby carriage, and perhaps a small loft for the screens and storm windows.

CHECK LIST FOR EASY LIVING

1. Step-saver kitchen throughout.
2. Sit-down space and storage for cookbooks and accounts.
3. Use dishwasher.
4. Use disposal unit.
5. Exhaust fan in kitchen.
6. Bundle delivery.
7. Pots and pans within easy reach.
8. Special storage for trays and platters.
9. Divided drawers for linen, silver, small utensils.
10. Chopping block at least 2′ wide—fixed or pull-out.
11. Sliding panel to dining room.
12. Swing-out refuse bin on back of cabinet door.
13. Chute to outdoor barrel for cans and bottles.

Here's a good thought for a trash chute. The regular type barrel may be removed when full and replaced. Barrel should be screened, of course.

14. Washable walls.
15. Good relation in work triangle—sink, refrigerator, range.
16. No traffic across triangle.
17. Space for kitchen eating.
18. No doors that obstruct work when open.
19. Sliding wall cabinet doors to avoid bumped heads.
20. Shelf for juicer in kitchen.
21. Swing-out shelf for electric mixer.
22. Can-opener on wall, magnetic type.
23. Desk in kitchen if no sit-down counter.
24. Plenty of storage cabinets with merry-go-rounds in corners.
25. Glass fronted cabinet doors for easy observation.
26. Ventilated bins for vegetables.
27. Component stoves.
28. Built-in refrigerator with storage cabinet above.
29. Stove to table cooking utensils.
30. Paper towels.
31. Paper cup dispenser.
32. Freezer.
33. Easy walk—garage to kitchen.
34. Acoustic ceiling where there is open plan.
35. Small built-in radio in kitchen.
36. Refrigerator door doesn't swing so it obstructs work.
37. Indoor barbecue in kitchen.
38. At least 9 lineal feet of counter.

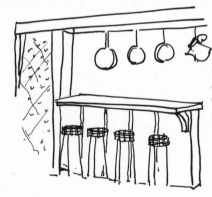

Counter-type eating spots serve when there is no room for table.

39. Lighted so there are no shaded work areas.
40. Resilient flooring, to be easier on feet.
41. Serving cart and no threshold between kitchen and dining area.
42. Double-sided cabinets.
43. Washer-dryer or washer and dryer.
44. Have telephone jack in kitchen.
45. In open kitchen-living room have 12″ baffle to hide used dishes.
46. Have plenty of natural light.
47. Be able to supervise play area through kitchen window.
48. Avoid hazardous corners, edges, knobs.
49. Have convenient kitchen scales.
50. Don't forget well located kitchen clock.
51. Ironer.
52. Plenty of towel racks for auxiliary drying—stockings, etc.
53. Full length mirror.
54. Recessed clothes hamper—in wall or under basin.
55. Exhaust fan.

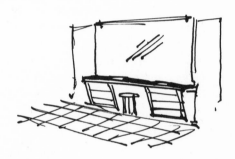

56. Counter-topped lavatory-dressing table with storage under.
57. Double counter-topped lavatories.
58. Grab bar next to tub.
59. Built-in magazine racks or shelf, and place for scales.
60. Shower-sized tub in half-bath.
61. Lavatory in bedroom closet as half-bath.
62. Good general and special lighting.
63. Ceiling light placed to shine inside closed shower curtains.
64. Easily cleaned walls.
65. Electric outlets, in safe place, for shaving, dryer, sunlamp, heatlamp.
66. Big medicine cabinet—sliding mirrored front.
67. Lockable medicine cabinet, against children.
68. Avoid window over tub.
69. Insulate bath walls to shield all sound.
70. Shut-offs for all faucets under fixtures.

71. Floor and counter top that do not stain easily.
72. Floor that does not get too slippery when wet.
73. Heater and light in bath ceiling.
74. Ample closets and deep enough.
75. To gain free floor area build in clothes hanging, drawers, shelves.
76. Bedroom-sitting room provision for parents.
77. Bedside telephone.
78. Master switch to floodlight exterior for apprehensive people.
79. Bedside magazine rack.
80. Good light for reading in bed.
81. Built-in radio.
82. Full length mirror.
83. Comfortable chair.
84. Call buzzer from old folks' bedroom.
85. Light in clothes closet and perhaps automatic door switch.
86. Beds so arranged that they are easy to make.
87. Easy access for serving cart during illness.
88. Use windows that can be washed easily.
89. Use easy to clean surfaces.
90. Use lights that do not require dusting.
91. Have everything on one floor.
92. Have one key for whole house.
93. Have dustproof moldings.
94. Automatic heating.
95. Air conditioning.
96. Intercommunicating system saves steps.
97. Garage door automatically controlled by switch in car.
98. Driveway with concealed coils or pipes to melt snow.
99. Night watchman which turns on lights automatically at dusk.
100. Mercury switches for quiet.
101. Window-type air conditioner may operate through floor.
102. Well insulated house.
103. Recessed radiation.
104. Garage near street.
105. No fuse cut-out box, use circuit-breakers.
106. Always remember easy upkeep.
107. Guard against summer sun through outsized windows.
108. Dehumidifier in cellar.
109. Have cellar light switch with telltale.
110. Adequate wiring for mechanical gear saves periodic trouble.
111. Racks for cellar storage—keeps it off floor and easy to reach.
112. With no cellar have minimum of 125 square feet in utility-storage room.
113. For barrel removal from cellar have stair-ramp combination.
114. To create bigger free area in living room use in-wall storage for—card tables, radio, T.V., books, drawer space, against wall storage for—desk, couch, table.
115. Where no summer living porch use multi-purpose garage.
116. Have at least 12 percent living floor area for *live* storage.
117. Adequate sound control between rooms by storage walls or insulation.
118. Attic fan for comfort.

TRY THIS FOR SIZE IN DOLLARS AND SENSE

THE QUESTION BEFORE THE HOUSE is, "What will it cost?" We'd like to answer that in exact figures but costs vary so from North to South and coast to coast that we can't give a definite price on any one house.

Now we don't recommend that anyone jump into anything and we believe you should have some indication of the cost. For this reason, we have indicated on each plan the number of square feet of living space on each house. This means the living area not including garages and porches. To arrive at an approximate cost, get a local builder to tell you the per square foot cost in his community which may be $10.00 to $15.00 depending on whether the house has a basement or not. Then multiply the cost per square foot by the number of square feet and you will arrive at the approximate cost of the house. In addition, an allowance should be made for garage and porches.

MONEY SAVERS AND IDEAS

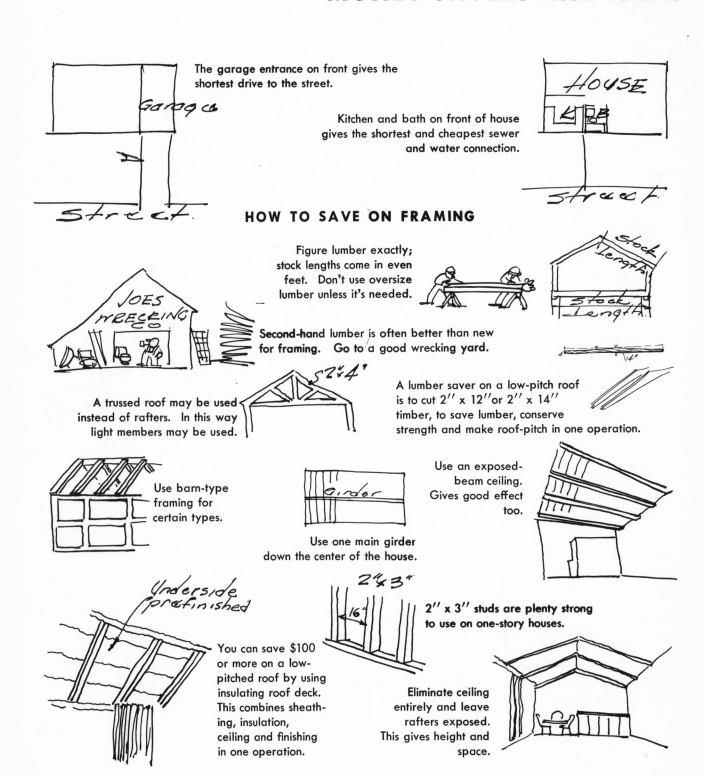

The **garage** entrance on front gives the shortest drive to the street.

Kitchen and bath on front of house gives the shortest and cheapest sewer and water connection.

HOW TO SAVE ON FRAMING

Figure lumber exactly; stock lengths come in even feet. Don't use oversize lumber unless it's needed.

Second-hand lumber is often better than new for framing. Go to a good wrecking **yard.**

A trussed roof may be used instead of rafters. In this way light members may be used.

A lumber saver on a low-pitch roof is to cut 2″ x 12″ or 2″ x 14″ timber, to save lumber, conserve strength and make roof-pitch in one operation.

Use barn-type framing for certain types.

Use one main **girder** down the center of the house.

Use an exposed-beam ceiling. Gives good effect too.

2″ x 3″ studs are plenty strong to use on one-story houses.

You can save $100 or more on a low-pitched roof by using insulating roof deck. This combines sheathing, insulation, ceiling and finishing in one operation.

Eliminate ceiling entirely and leave rafters exposed. This gives height and space.

42

HOW TO SAVE ON WALLS

Vertical boarding used without sheathing gives added strength plus economy. Note how boards are placed — not a board and batten wall. Looks well in cedar.

WALL PLAN.

A brick wall laid 2″ thick costs but little more than wood. It also saves 4″ in depth of house over a standard brick job. Lay it like any brick veneer, but on edge.

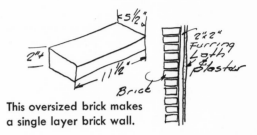

This oversized brick makes a single layer brick wall.

16″ 96″ Insulating strips / *Stud* / *Wood shingles* / *clip*

This scheme does the sheathing and shingling in one operation. It saves a lot of labor.

2′-0″ plywood

2′-0″ wide sheets of plywood laid like clapboards. Sheathing may be omitted. It gives an unusual wall treatment.

Insulating board used in place of sheathing saves money. Clapboards work better than shingles.

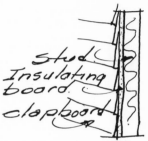

stud / *Insulating board.* / *clapboard*

A good money saving material for side walls is ready colored asbestos board. It's inexpensive, easy to install and does not require painting.

A board and batten wall is most decorative and may be made in a single layer. If pine or other wood is used inside, the studs may be spaced much wider than is normal — a great dollar saver.

Stud / *Felt* / *Ins* / *one layer vertical pine Battens over joints vertical pine inside*

Nowadays you can even buy a prefabricated chimney. Saves space — saves dollars.

Exterior plywood may be used in the same way in one layer. With battens every 16″.

A money saver on a chimney.

Bound pipe / *Brick*

The cheaper grades of plywood or standard composition board may be used for sheathing. Gypsum sheathing is the least expensive but provides no nailing as does plywood.

HOW TO SAVE ON ROOFS

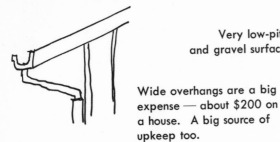

Very low-pitched roofs with tar and gravel surface are the cheapest.

Wide overhangs are a big expense — about $200 on a house. A big source of upkeep too.

Slate-surface roll roofing is far from beautiful, but is a dollar saver and will last for years.

You can save a lot by leaving off gutters, leaders, and dry wells. Saves $200 to $300.

No Gutters or leaders

Use unpainted wooden shingles to weather. Saves paint. Use pre-painted trim.

Here's a good stunt for a slate roof: stretch the exposure by using felt between courses.

Strip Felt between courses.

HOW TO SAVE ON WINDOWS

A good stunt is to use fixed glass with louvers for vents.

Louvre Fixed Glass

Cellar windows used in series for modern treatment.

Fixed Glass — *Louvr*

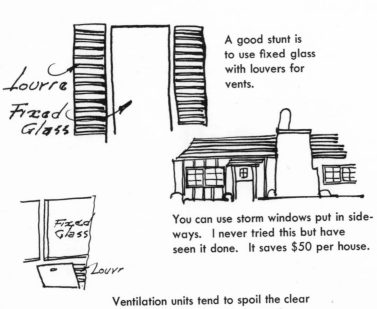

You can use storm windows put in sideways. I never tried this but have seen it done. It saves $50 per house.

Did you ever stop to think what curtains cost? This hall window bright with plants needs no hangings — can be used as a room divider, too.

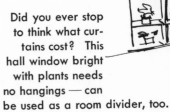

Ventilation units tend to spoil the clear sweep of plate-glass windows. Louvers below the windows are the answer to this.

44

HOW TO SAVE ON DOORS

The biggest saving you can make on doors is to omit them. Make a big closet like this with contents screened from view.

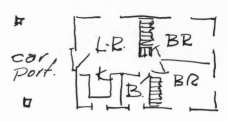

See what I mean by omitting doors — only 4 doors in this house.

Eliminate all finish possible. For a modern job you need none around doors and windows.

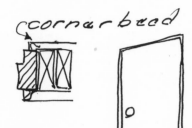

Stock blinds are here used as louvered doors to shut off dual-use den-living room.

If you use trim, make it stock. I often use stock window stops for trim and base.

A good idea to make a Dutch door is to saw a stock door in two and rabbet it. Saves maybe $25.

Here's a hinge that just screws on. Requires no mortising; saves $50 ± per house.

Flush doors unpainted make an economical treatment.

Use door hardware that can be put on by boring two holes.

Metal door frames are dollar savers.

HOW TO SAVE ON FLOORS

Cement may be plain or marked off in squares with redwood in joints for a special deal.

Carpet over one-layer plywood makes for luxury at low cost.

Cement floors are the cheapest. They may be covered with carpet.

Asphalt tile is a great money saver.

Flagstone in cement should not be too expensive.

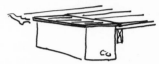

Where wall-to-wall carpets are used this insulating board base saves money and provides resilience.

HOW TO SAVE ON HEAT

A unit heater that suspends from ceiling will heat a small house. House must be well-insulated and partitions stop short of ceilings.

The same sort of heater may be rigged up with ducts.

A single floor heater will heat a small house — good for basementless houses with crawl space.

Wall heaters, opening into two rooms, are low in cost. Fit in a normal partition.

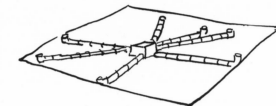

A very low cost way of installing hot air heat is to bury the ducts under the slab. Ducts are made of cement, cost about $100 to install.

Electric panel heaters are costly to operate but are low in first cost, require no chimney or heater room. Take up no space.

A prefabricated plenum chamber is used with great saving to distribute hot air in an underslab heating system.

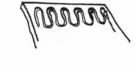

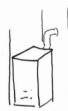

Gas heaters are cheaper to install than oil and where gas is cheap, are economical to use. Small size will fit in closet.

Radiant coils in floor slab save a lot of cutting for radiators or ducts — give uniform heat, but slightly warm on the feet. Factory formed coils save money.

This wall furnace requires no flue, no chimney, no heater space. It will fit any room like a radiator, vents through wall. A good idea for cellarless houses where space is at a premium.

A counter-top hot water heater used with radiant coils in the slab is a good thought. It fits in the kitchen.

Electric cable hidden in the ceiling heats the house by radiant heat. Saves heater, chimney flue, heater space, radiators and pipes. Easy to install but running cost is higher than most fuels except where electricity is cheap. Just a flip of the switch and the heat is on.

FIREPLACES

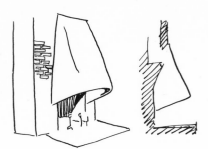

A steel fireplace hood is a good touch, be the house modern or traditional.

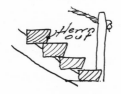

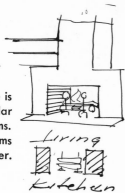

A two-way fireplace is cheaper than the regular type and serves two rooms. Also it makes the rooms look bigger.

STAIRS

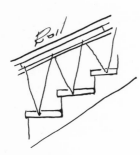

Use open stair with cord lacing instead of baluster.

A solid beam stair, made of short-length low cost timber.

A ship's ladder stair to a second floor balcony makes an interesting and amusing economy.

GENERAL IDEAS

20 years and more ago, I predicted that some one would invent a building material which could be used for most everything, mainly partitions, all in one layer. Now they've made it — it's like a sandwich of two layers of gypsum board with a cellular paper core much like a flush door core. It's light, durable, usable, and about ½ price of standard partitions.

Chipboard is a textured wall board made of pressed cedar chips. Has a rich texture when finished — low in cost.

Here's a new ceramic tile adhesive which can bond real ceramic tile to any surface — saves $50 on a bath.

There's a new plastic finish for counters that brushes on and looks like glass when completed. Eliminates need for other counter surfacing.

A 20-lb. plastic bathtub that a child can lift saves $5 — wears well and looks well. Builds in like a regular tub.

A corrugated plastic makes a good translucent windbreak for terrace.

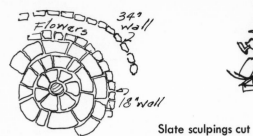

Flowers wall 34" 18" wall

A prefabricated metal bulkhead. Saves quite a bit.

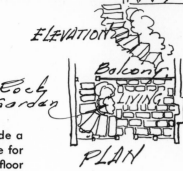

ELEVATION
Rock Garden
Balcony
LIVING
PLAN

Slate sculpings cut at the quarry make a good terrace.

A rock garden inside a house gives a chance for garden steps to second floor balcony.

post Lattice or split cedar

A screen fence made of woven lattice or cedar makes a good garden screen; can be curved or bent to suit shape of terrace.

Flower box built in at end of stone wall.

Post 1" Steel Pin concrete

An idea for fence posts which won't rot out.

DO IT YOURSELF

Lay your own cement slab.

Lay out your own foundation and stake out the house.

2"x4"

I know many a young man who has prebuilt his own wall frames and erected them with the help of a friend.

Apply insulating sheathing to house.

Apply shingle backer and shingles.

It's no job at all to put up the modern type of ceiling tiles.

PART TWO

KITCHENS. The living room has moved right into the kitchen, or vice versa, as attested by the following sketches. If Madam is going to spend all her time in the culinary department, she doesn't want to feel lonely. The man of the house can loll here in slippers, with pipe in his mouth.

Natural materials naturally used are the theme, and although the treatments are similar, they run the gamut from traditional to modern. Whatever your choice, they are all downright livable.

A free interpretation of the old colonial kitchen with hand hewn beams and paneling and chimney of old brick.

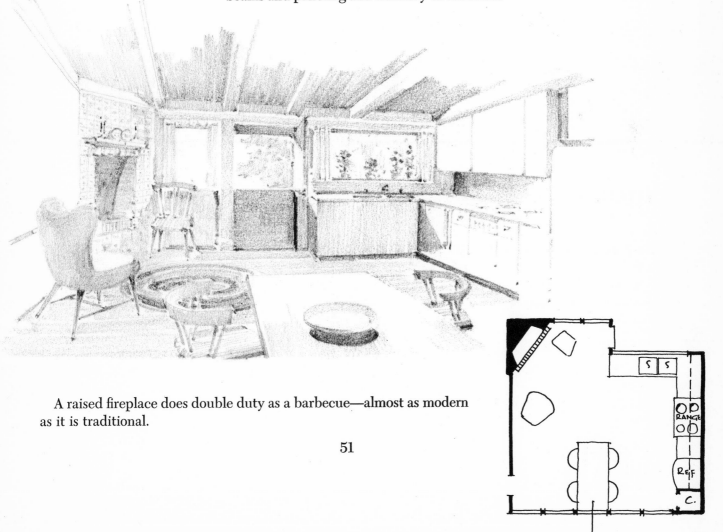

A raised fireplace does double duty as a barbecue—almost as modern as it is traditional.

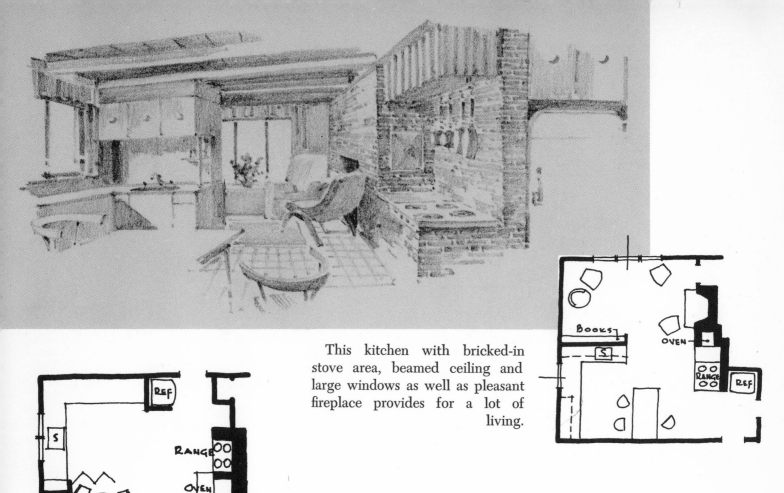

This kitchen with bricked-in stove area, beamed ceiling and large windows as well as pleasant fireplace provides for a lot of living.

The raised stone fireplace and beamed ceiling might be a bit of yesterday but the big windows and efficient work center are a bit of today.

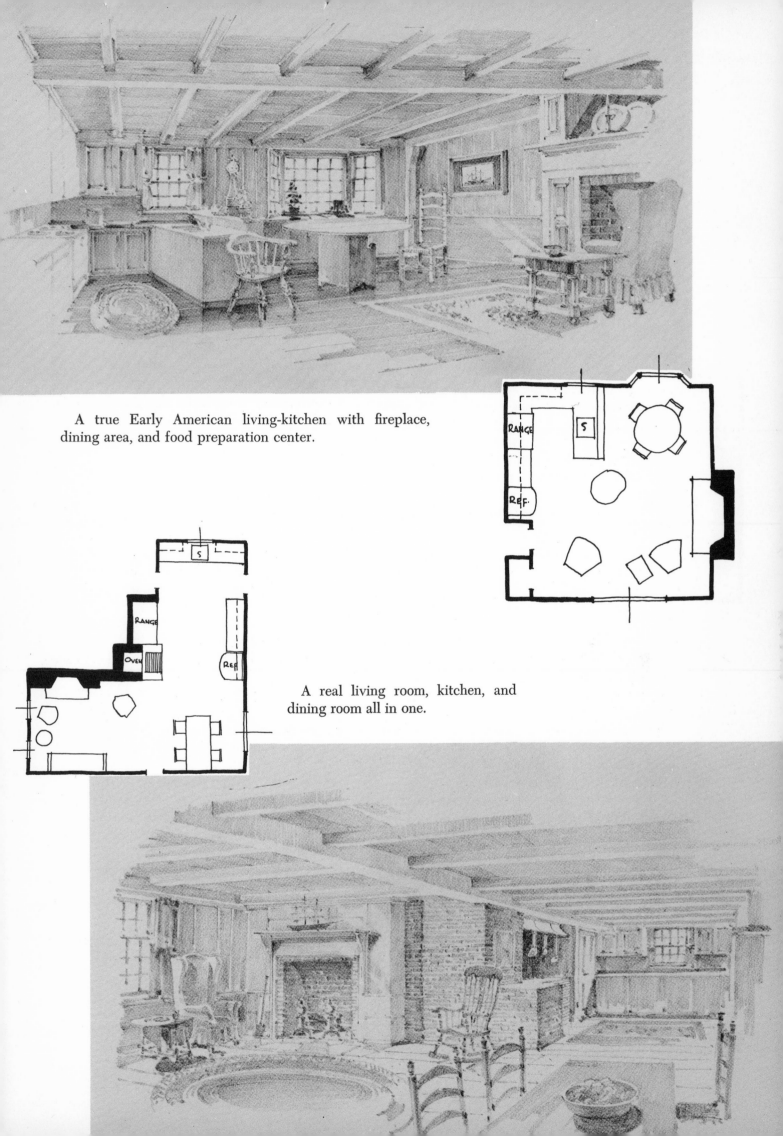

A true Early American living-kitchen with fireplace, dining area, and food preparation center.

A real living room, kitchen, and dining room all in one.

SINCE ABOUT THE CHEAPEST little house you can build costs $10,000.00, how in the world can you do it for $5,000.00? Well, the only way you can do it is to leave out half of everything. Sounds funny but it's not as funny as it sounds.

Suppose you take a house—you leave out the first floor, leave out the second floor, leave out the walls. The attic and the basement are the two cheapest parts of the house—well, use them.

Then you get a house that looks like a tent—like this.

Side walls 4' high of stone or blocks. To save money further, drop the floor into the ground 4' except on one side (so you have no side wall cost). This is a big money saver because the house is so easy to heat that you can do it with a space heater which is low in cost. Yearly heating bill on a little house of this sort should be under $100.00, maybe $50.00.

For windows, use some fixed glass in both ends—like this.

Make lovely sunny rooms.

Make a big combination living-kitchen—like this.

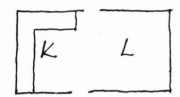

Put in two bedrooms and bath and a little balcony over, which looks like this. It can be reached by a ship's ladder and can be used for an emergency bedroom or storage.

For luxury, put in a fireplace if you wish or save $200.00 if you want to.

Use single layer partitions to make closets and walls.

Use self-supporting plank and beam roof to save money. Let natural wood be exposed. Use open shelves in kitchen part.

Use no painting except what you can do yourself.

No finish except kitchen. Here use stock stove and cabinet plus stock sink and cabinet and stock shelves.

Use plank and beam floor over bedroom. Living room exposed to ceiling.

Use a painted cement floor with plenty of rugs.

Of course you have to do a lot of your own labor.

Laugh clown, laugh, but it makes a cozy house and I refer you to the large sketch and plan to see how really livable it is.

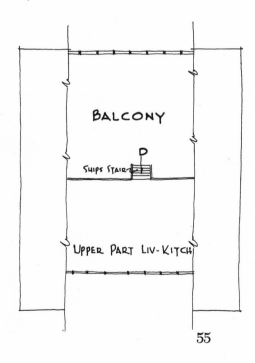

BALCONY

Ships Stair

Upper Part Liv-Kitch

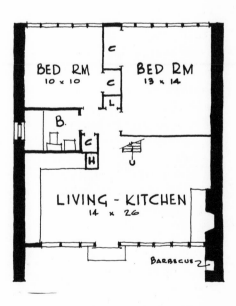

BED RM
10 x 10

BED RM
13 x 14

B.

LIVING - KITCHEN
14 x 26

BARBECUE

692 square feet

55

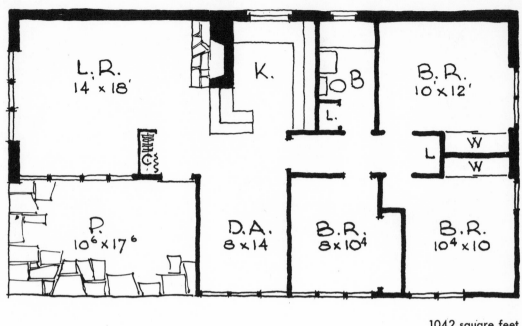

1042 square feet

This little house is built into a bank radically reducing building costs.
Heating and maintenance will be at a minimum.

This is a far cry from the old-fashioned summer cottage with its mixture of worn Victorian and wicker furniture and jigsaw work galloping all around the miniature front porch.

This is no camp though. It's good for summer or year round. It's heated with a floor furnace which, with a super insulation job, will keep it warm in tough weather.

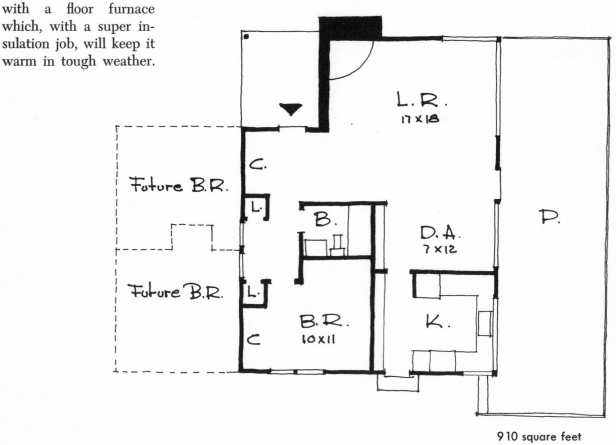

910 square feet

This house is literally built right into the ground. Facing south, it becomes a solar house in the true sense of the word. Its lines are clean and vibrant with wide expanses of glass.

It is a small house yet provides a wealth of space, really six rooms, and it can be built for an idiotically low price even in these times.

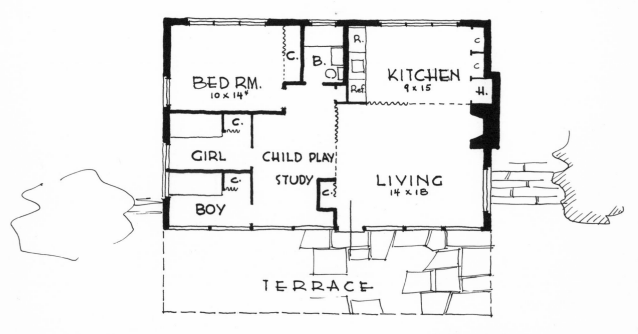

1000 square feet

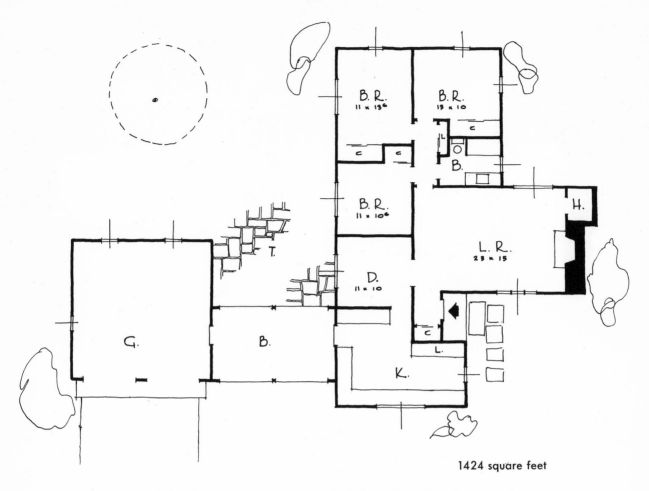

B. R.
11 x 13⁶

B. R.
13 x 10

B. R.
11 x 10⁶

L. R.
23 x 15

H.

D.
11 x 10

T.

G.

B.

K.

1424 square feet

This house is not just a scaled-down bit of architectural history. It is an outgrowth of the times; natural materials naturally used.

The house has low sprawling lines typical of the transitional house of today. It has large windows with a good chance for outdoor living. For a house with so little hall space it has remarkably good circulation.

This is a tiny attenuated house. It can be very low in cost but often suffers from hidebound building laws: it can be framed with light members and be remarkably strong but building laws specify certain minimums which would more adequately apply to much larger houses.

Note the minimum of hall space. A third bedroom may be easily added.

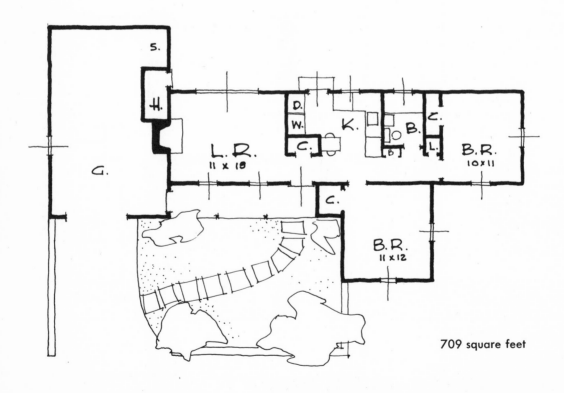

709 square feet

People like houses that show that their beginnings were in the past. They prefer attractive houses—I won't use the word pretty, with its "cute" connotations.

The living, dining and kitchen space may be thrown into one with the chimney acting as a room divider.

The house follows no particular precedent. It's really modern but it would fit in readily with a group of traditional houses.

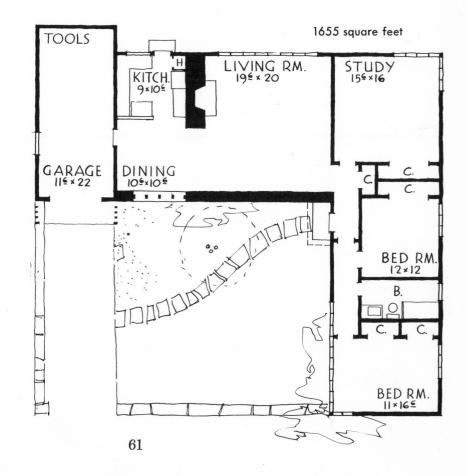

61

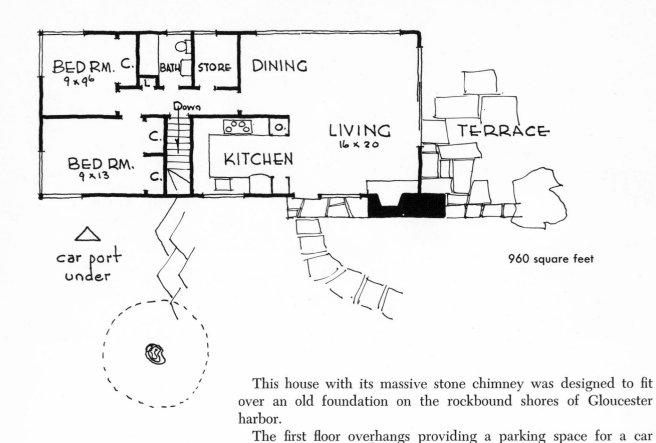

BED RM. C.
9 x 96

BATH STORE DINING

Down

C.

BED RM.
9 x 13

C.

KITCHEN

LIVING
16 x 20

TERRACE

car port
under

960 square feet

This house with its massive stone chimney was designed to fit over an old foundation on the rockbound shores of Gloucester harbor.

The first floor overhangs providing a parking space for a car underneath. Living room, dining room, and kitchen open into one large area. The storeroom can be used as a tiny bedroom since there is plenty of storage space below.

One often gets tired of an all wood house and large window areas seem to call for rugged materials such as stone and rough siding. The walls here are made of quarried stone ranging in color from purple to grey and green, and of rough sawn vertical boards of cedar or pine.

It was quite easy to design a miniature house in the colonial style but it is much harder to achieve the same charm in the so-called ranch house of rectangular shape.

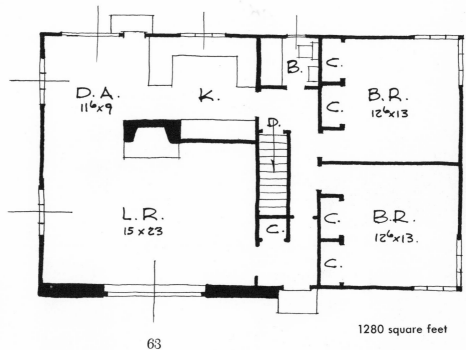

1280 square feet

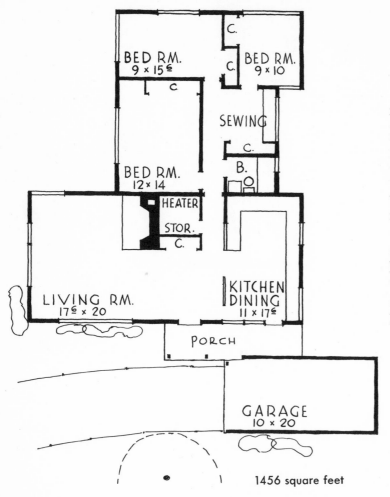

BED RM.
9 x 15⁶

C.

C.

BED RM.
9 x 10

SEWING

C.

B.

BED RM.
12 x 14

HEATER

STOR.

C.

LIVING RM.
17⁶ x 20

KITCHEN
DINING
11 x 17⁶

PORCH

GARAGE
10 x 20

1456 square feet

This simple and serene little house is designed for a narrow lot. Its low-pitched roofs, grouped windows and large chimney give it a comfortable look which will live well. The walls are of rough sawn boards, white-washed, and the roof is covered with rough cedar shakes.

For a small house this has a lot of space with its big living-dining-kitchen area and its three bedrooms. The sewing room is an added dividend with its big window and large linen closet.

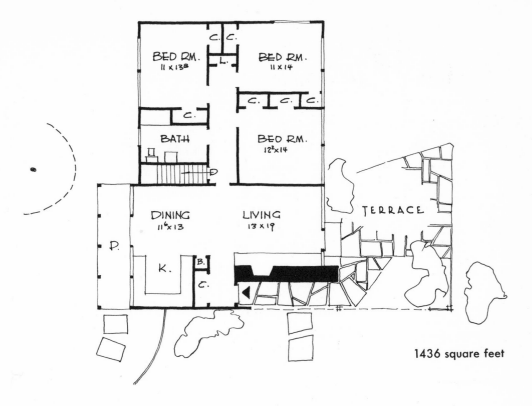

1436 square feet

There's nothing I like better than a massive chimney and I won't settle for less even on a contemporary house. While this house doesn't bow down to any one school of thought, it's as modern as tomorrow with its one-way low-pitched roof.

Don't think just because we made the sketch in green and chinese white that it has to be a white house. It can be of weathered wood and stone. No. 2 cedar or pecky cypress would be good too.

Taste is an elusive thing. It's a matter of suitability. It's more a question of appropriateness. It's a most natural thing to combine the materials you like in a house. Then it will reflect your personality.

If you like big chimneys and long low lines even in a little house, here it is. Timbers around the carport along with the stone give a rugged note to the exterior. Across the lot it looks big but when placed endways to the street it will go on a minimum sized lot.

890 square feet

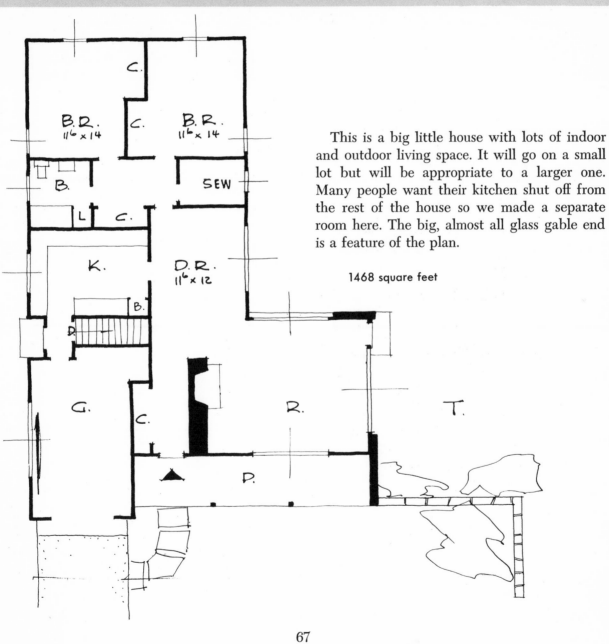

This is a big little house with lots of indoor and outdoor living space. It will go on a small lot but will be appropriate to a larger one. Many people want their kitchen shut off from the rest of the house so we made a separate room here. The big, almost all glass gable end is a feature of the plan.

1468 square feet

67

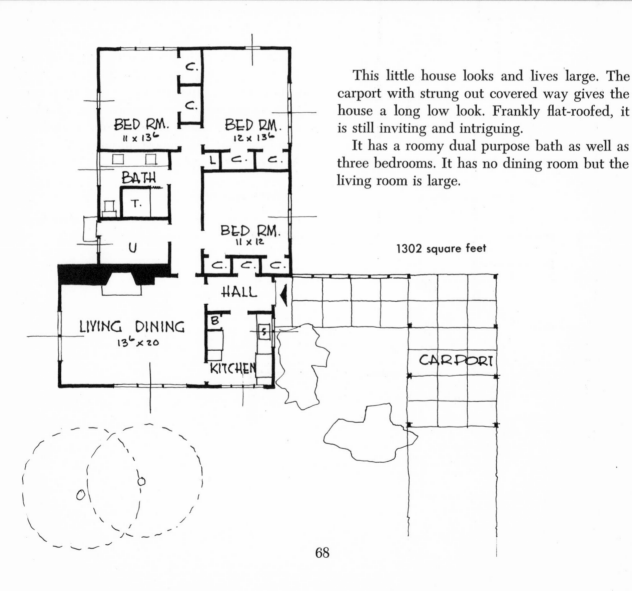

This little house looks and lives large. The carport with strung out covered way gives the house a long low look. Frankly flat-roofed, it is still inviting and intriguing.

It has a roomy dual purpose bath as well as three bedrooms. It has no dining room but the living room is large.

1302 square feet

This rambling one-story house takes its details from the colonial and its long low sweeping lines from the real ranch houses of the west. It might be called a happy marriage of the ranch house and colonial.

Sparkling white, the stone chimney gives it a Midas touch. It really is not large but all the rooms are spacious and you can easily get in an extra bath if you wish.

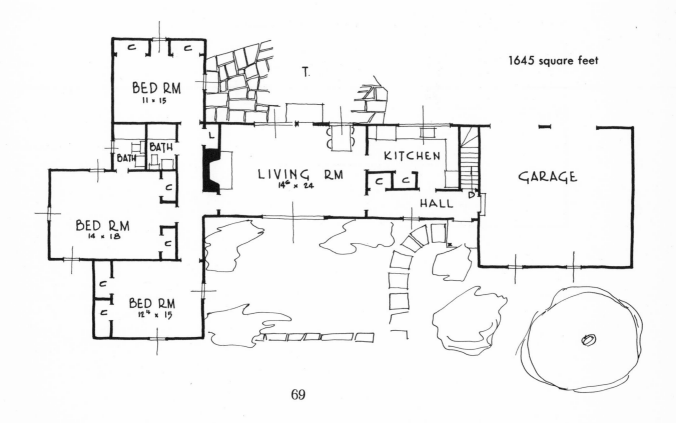

1645 square feet

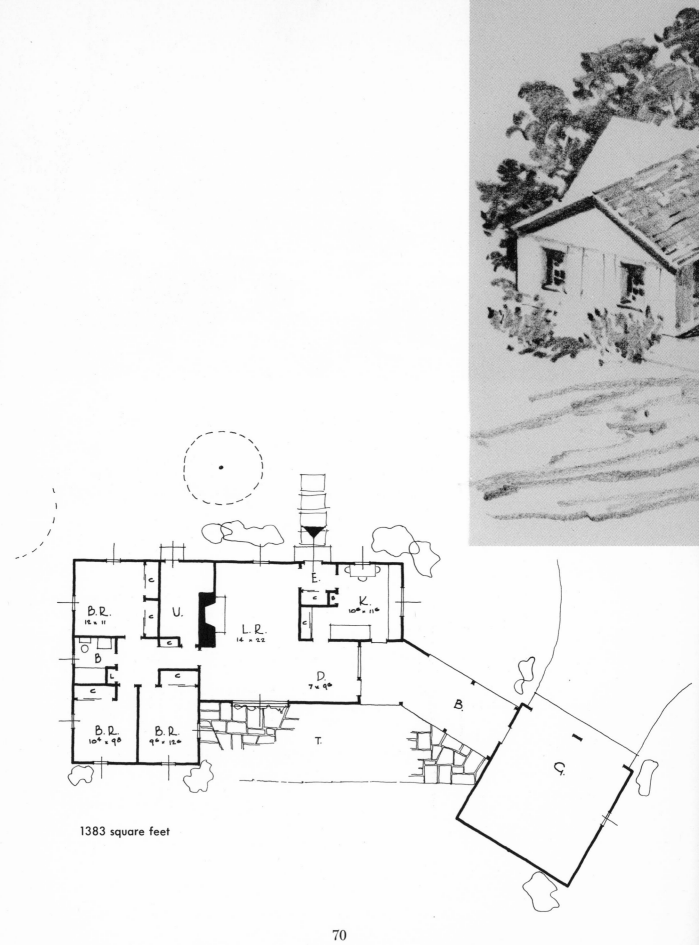

B.R.
12 x 11

U.

C

C

C

C

B

L

C

C

B.R.
10⁴ x 9⁸

B.R.
9⁶ x 12⁶

L.R.
14 x 22

E.

C

B

K.
10⁸ x 11⁶

D.
7 x 9⁸

T.

B.

G.

1383 square feet

This house looks informal, is informal and is easy to live in informally. It is good-looking and efficient.

The walk way to the garage makes it look long, low and rangy.

A screened-off door opens into the utility room.

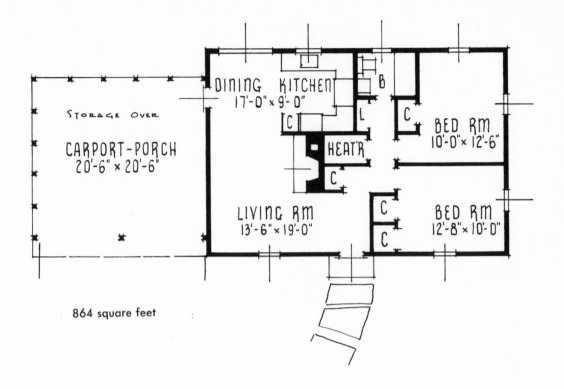

STORAGE OVER

CARPORT-PORCH
20'-6" x 20'-6"

DINING | KITCHEN
17'-0" x 9'-0"

B

C

L

C

HEAT'R

BED RM
10'-0" x 12'-6"

C

LIVING RM
13'-6" x 19'-0"

C

C

BED RM
12'-8" x 10'-0"

864 square feet

There are so many people that like the simple symmetrical lines of the little Cape Cod house. Frankly quaint, cozy and unafraid, this little house sits behind its wall and picket fence giving built-in privacy.

Plenty of storage space is available in the attic and over the carport ceiling.

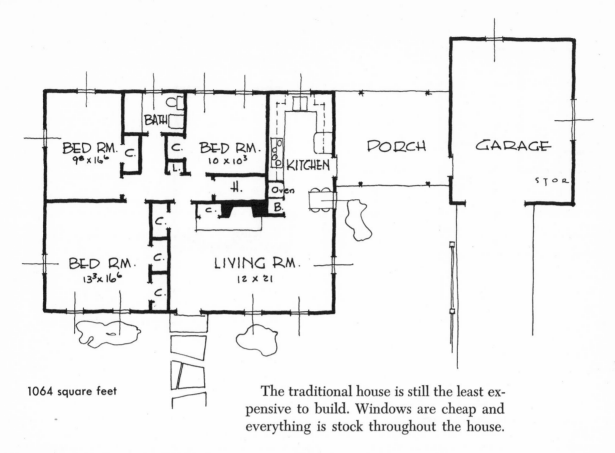

1064 square feet

The traditional house is still the least expensive to build. Windows are cheap and everything is stock throughout the house.

The combined living-dining-kitchen gives a whole lot of space in one area. Although there is no hall the circulation area hugs the living room wall.

There is no cellar provided but a stair can easily be put in the space allocated for heater.

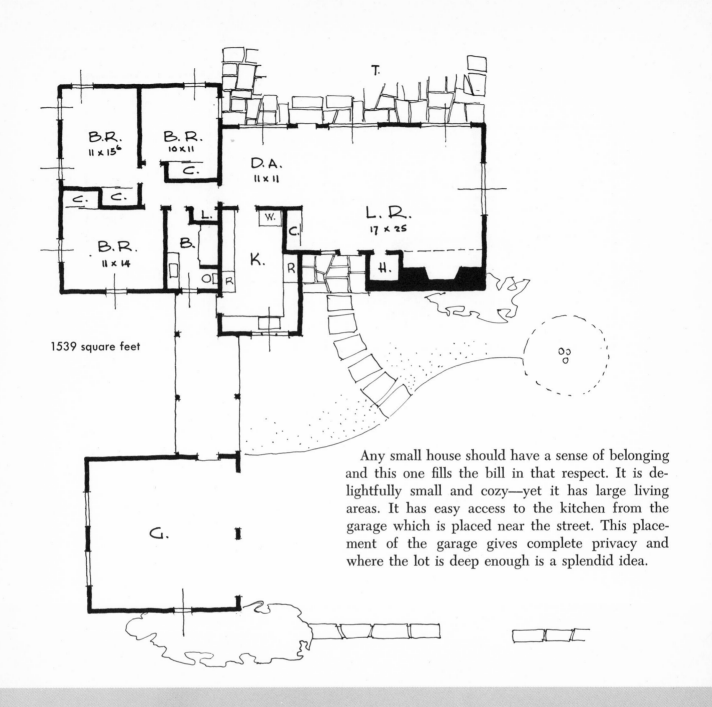

B.R.
11 x 15⁶

B.R.
10 x 11

C.

C.

C.

B.R.
11 x 14

B.

L.

O.

R.

D.A.
11 x 11

W.

K.

R.

C.

T.

L.R.
17 x 25

C.

H.

1539 square feet

G.

Any small house should have a sense of belonging and this one fills the bill in that respect. It is delightfully small and cozy—yet it has large living areas. It has easy access to the kitchen from the garage which is placed near the street. This placement of the garage gives complete privacy and where the lot is deep enough is a splendid idea.

This sinuous smooth-working angled plan is found in this long low lanky house. It's informal. It hugs the land. It fits *anywhere*. It is traditional and transitional all in one. The large open living area is modern too.

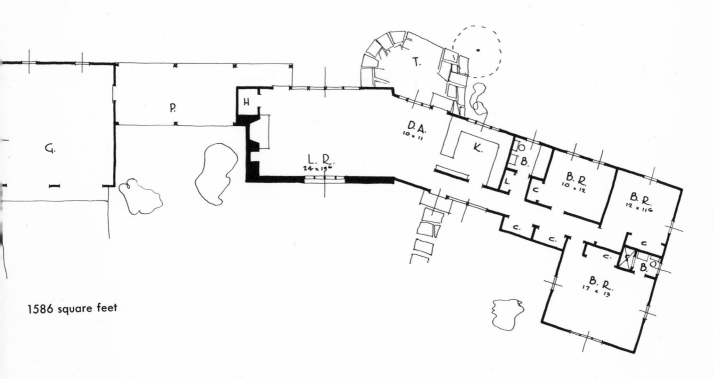

1586 square feet

Patio living in good weather is all the rage in this country now. Instead of going to the country on a weekend, you stay home and let the kids paddle in the lily pond on the terrace. Outdoor cookouts are fun or just plain lazing in the sun.

This house has a big kitchen, a big living room with dining area and three bedrooms and two baths and plenty of closet space.

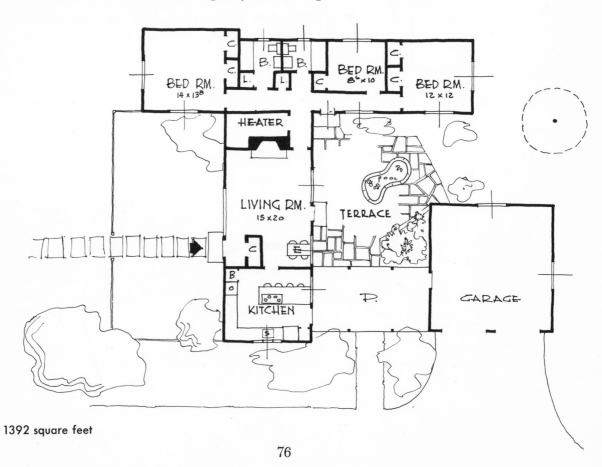

1392 square feet

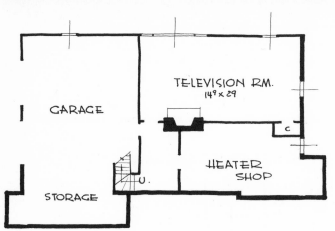

This house, designed for a sloping corner lot, has the accent on charm, comfort, and economy. It packs a great deal of space into a relatively small area. It has the intimate personal scale of the one-story colonial houses. Large windows serve the living room on the rear. It should have hand split shingles on the roof.

The house has an excellent plan and good circulation. There is a minimum of hall space. It has easy access to garage from the kitchen. A large family room or television room is located on the lower level.

It has two baths and seven rooms altogether which puts it in the classification of a large house.

2361 square feet

This is a house for living in the present tense. The dramatic use of glass in the living room terrace wall makes it as modern as a morning paper. It's easy on indoor-outdoor living and terrace meals.

Actually there are three bedrooms, two baths, and a study area which may be shut off, which makes this a large house.

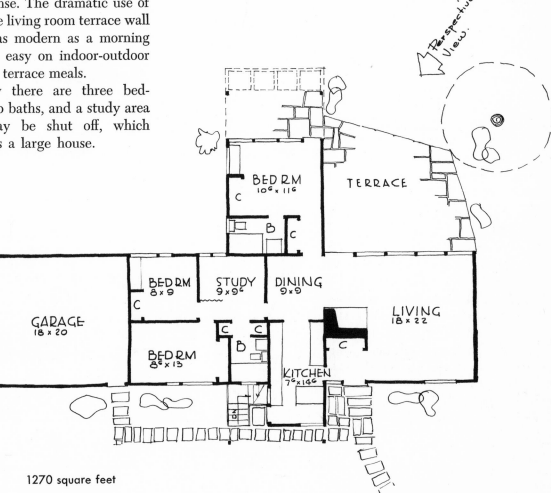

Perspective View.

BED RM
10⁶ x 11⁶

TERRACE

BED RM
8 x 9

STUDY
9 x 9⁶

DINING
9 x 9

LIVING
18 x 22

GARAGE
18 x 20

BED RM
8⁶ x 13

KITCHEN
7⁶ x 14⁶

1270 square feet

78

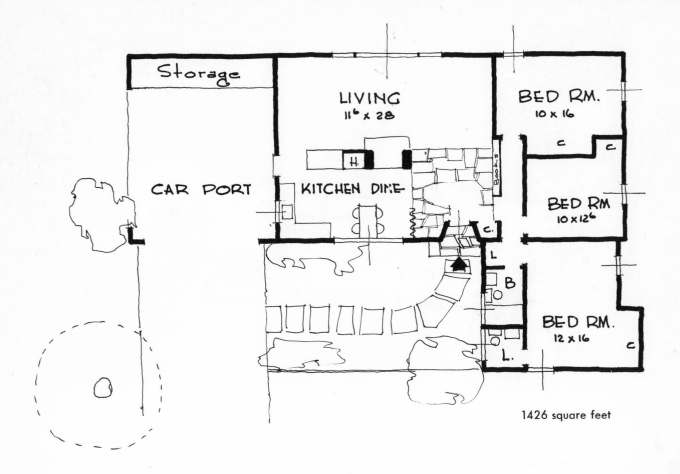

Storage

LIVING
11⁶ x 28

BED RM.
10 x 16

CAR PORT

KITCHEN DINE

Books

c   c

BED RM
10 x 12⁶

H.

c.

L

B

BED RM.
12 x 16

L.

c

1426 square feet

Here we have all the features of a big house: three bedrooms and one and one-half baths, for one thing; a big sweeping vista of the living room as one enters the front door, and then a long, long living room.

The low comfortable exterior with its oversize chimney is interesting.

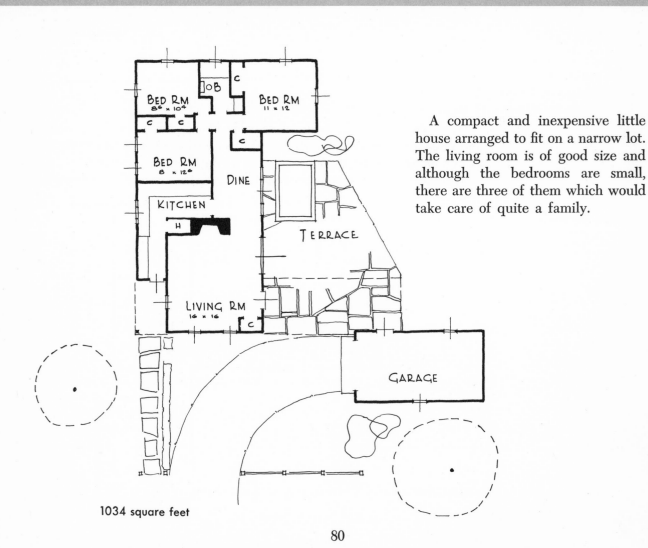

BED RM
8⁶ x 10⁴

B

C

BED RM
11 x 12

BED RM
8 x 12⁶

DINE

KITCHEN

H

TERRACE

LIVING RM
16 x 16

GARAGE

A compact and inexpensive little house arranged to fit on a narrow lot. The living room is of good size and although the bedrooms are small, there are three of them which would take care of quite a family.

1034 square feet

This house is a combination of white painted shingles, vertical boards and stone.

For all its appearance of diversity it is really a simple house. Just a T-shaped plan.

This house lives well—is suited to indoor-outdoor dining. It has three bedrooms and two baths as well as a living room, dining area and kitchen.

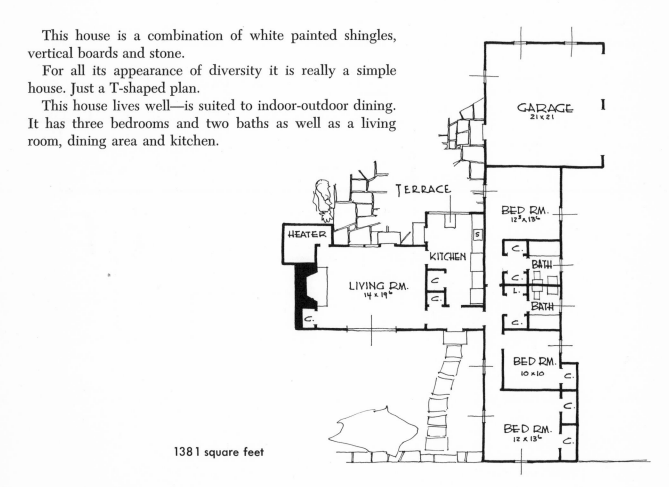

1381 square feet

81

The long low graceful lines give this house repose. Here is a smooth-working contemporary home without any sacrifice of the mellow charm and color of the traditional. Note the two baths and plenty of cross-ventilation.

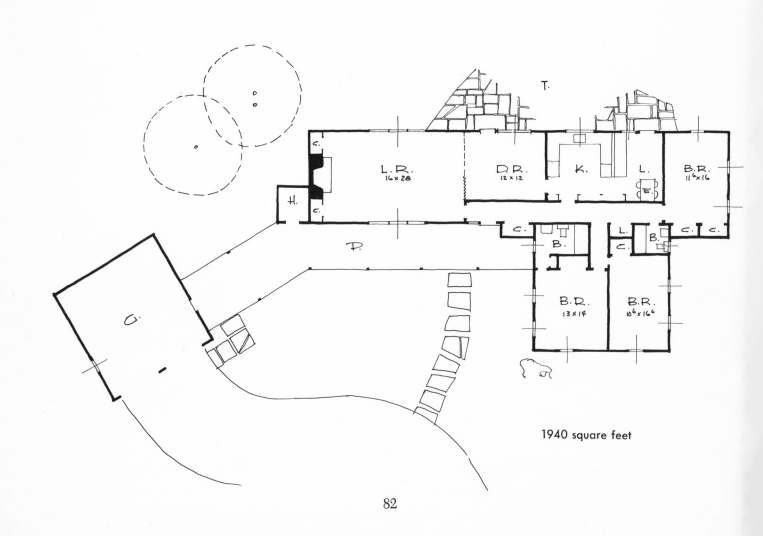

1940 square feet

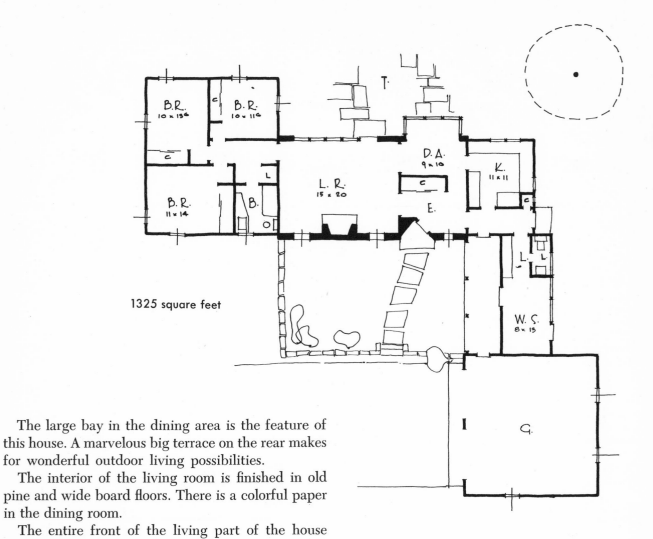

1325 square feet

The large bay in the dining area is the feature of this house. A marvelous big terrace on the rear makes for wonderful outdoor living possibilities.

The interior of the living room is finished in old pine and wide board floors. There is a colorful paper in the dining room.

The entire front of the living part of the house is of stone.

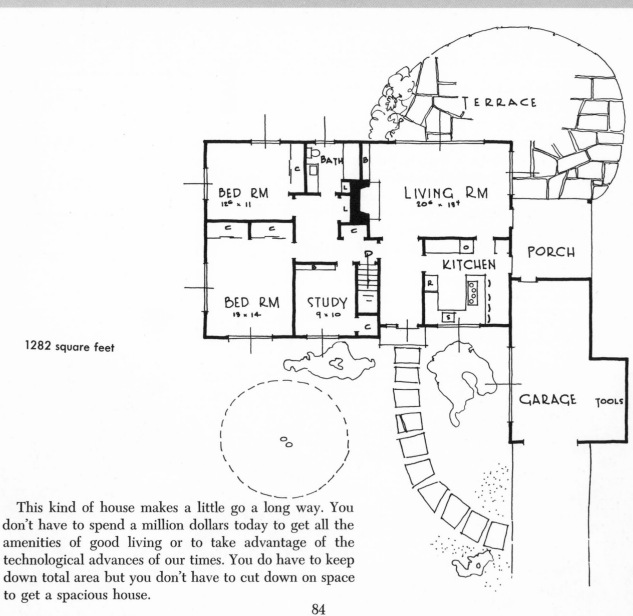

1282 square feet

This kind of house makes a little go a long way. You don't have to spend a million dollars today to get all the amenities of good living or to take advantage of the technological advances of our times. You do have to keep down total area but you don't have to cut down on space to get a spacious house.

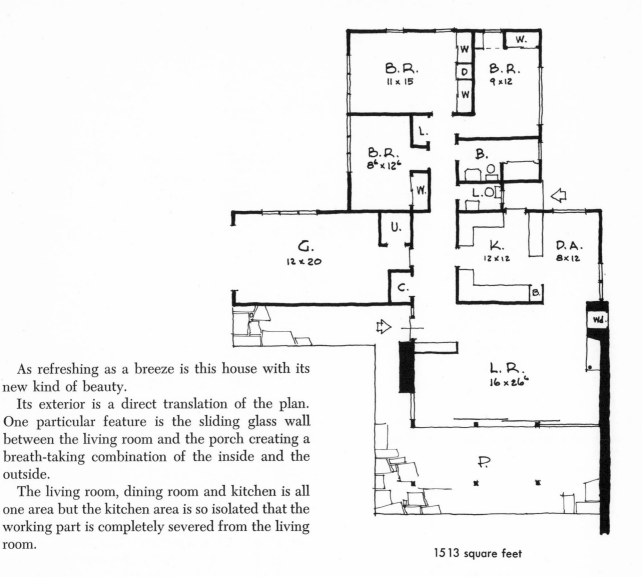

As refreshing as a breeze is this house with its new kind of beauty.

Its exterior is a direct translation of the plan. One particular feature is the sliding glass wall between the living room and the porch creating a breath-taking combination of the inside and the outside.

The living room, dining room and kitchen is all one area but the kitchen area is so isolated that the working part is completely severed from the living room.

1513 square feet

This house looks like a winged bird with rooms sprouting in three directions. There's a good reason for it too. It was built on a peninsula extending into a lagoon with a breath-taking view of the Atlantic beyond.

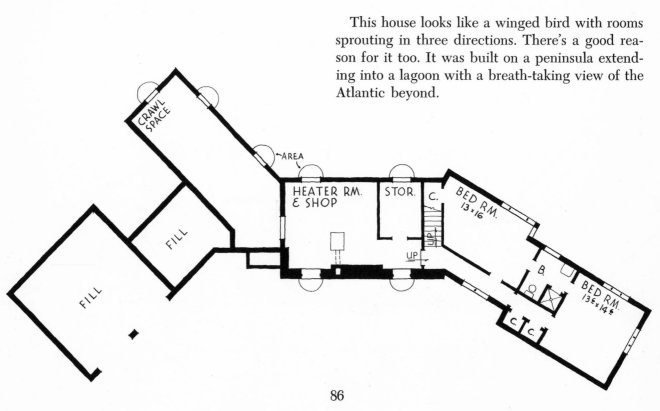

86

The kitchen was placed at that particular angle so that a less attractive view might be screened. The bedroom wing is so placed that the windows face onto the quiet blue waters of the little inland harbor and to the cliffs beyond.

The house is fitted to the contours of the lot like a glove.

The living room and dining room are all one, and give a tremendous open area. Up two steps from the living room is the owner's suite of two bedrooms and bath. One of the bedrooms is used as a study.

Downstairs there are two bedrooms and bath well above the steeply sloping grade.

Some houses we make square and stress the matter of economy. In some we stress circulation. In this house we stressed the view and the contours of the land.

Since the view was toward the north, windows were needed on the south to catch the sunlight. This explains the one-room-deep plan.

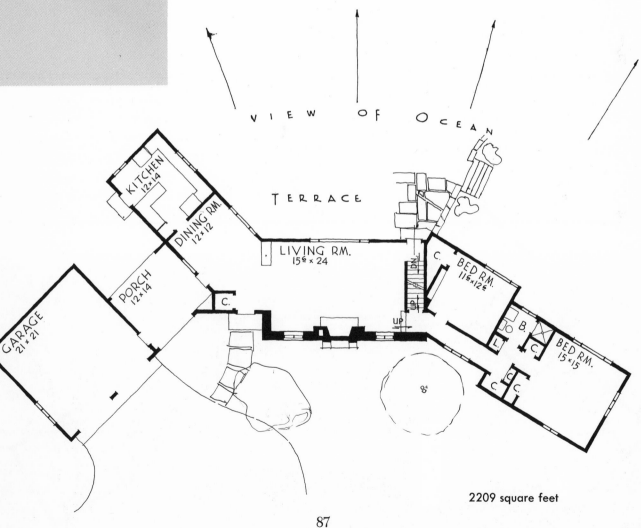

2209 square feet

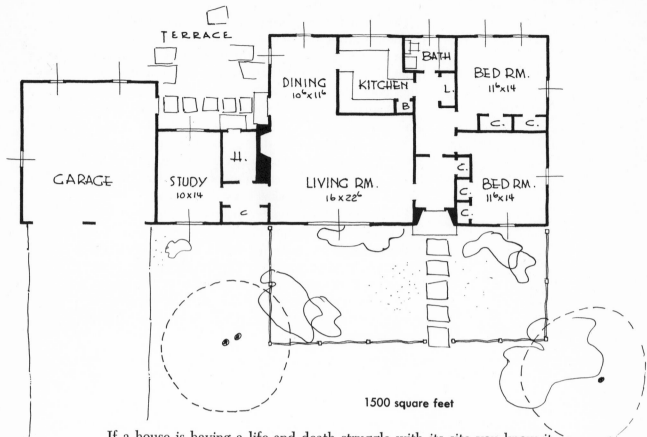

1500 square feet

If a house is having a life and death struggle with its site you know it will never be at peace with the world. A house should grow out of the site and have a warm relationship therewith. That does not mean that any house cannot avail itself of the enormous technical benefits of our time. I like houses that have a belonging look and this one has that quality. The plan is simple, direct and easy to build. It shows no basement but it is easy to put in. What's more, with a stair to the second floor you can get two bedrooms upstairs.

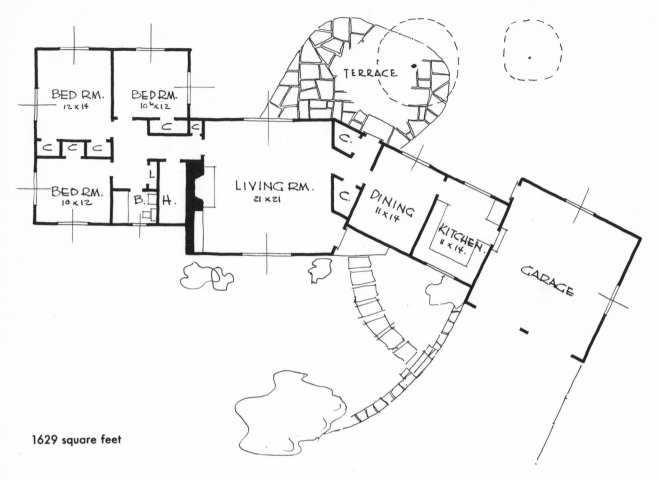

BED RM.
12 x 14

BED RM.
10⁶ x 12

C C

C C C

BED RM.
10 x 12

B. H.

L

LIVING RM.
21 x 21

TERRACE

C.

C.

DINING
11 x 14

KITCHEN.
11 x 14.

GARAGE

1629 square feet

This carefree small house takes wings, as it were. We try to make all these houses as flexible as we can. This one can be built backwards or forwards. The terrace entrance can easily become the front door. The old familiar materials make up the exterior. The stone end with its big chimney is a nice feature.

CROMBIE

Lots of old Cape Cod houses had a little main house with ells rambling all over the place. The main unit is a simple, symmetrical mass, setting close to the ground with a mammoth brick chimney centered on this unit. The whole composition makes an eye-catching bit of scenery, and gives the opportunity for almost any variety of plans although it takes a bit of skill and ingenuity to achieve an ideal result. Even large windows discreetly used are quite possible although an extensive use of plate glass would surely dictate another kind of a house.

The house shown above combines all the features mentioned plus a wonderful living-kitchen with fireplace. There are three bedrooms and two baths as well as living room, dining room, study and kitchen. The front is of clapboards painted white and the sides and rear of shingles left to weather naturally.

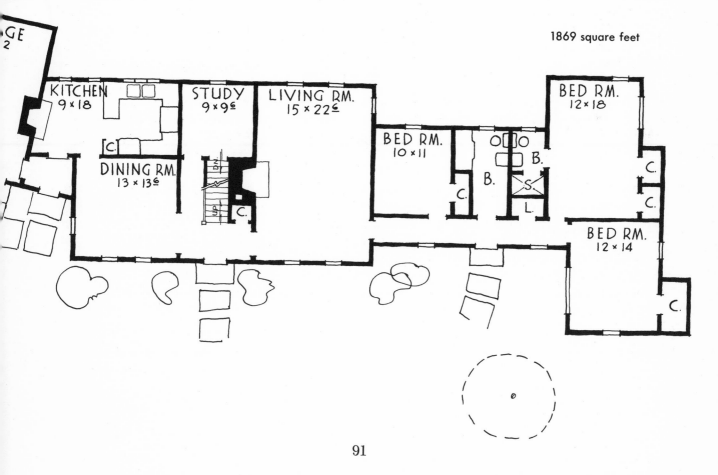

1869 square feet

GE
2

KITCHEN
9 × 18

STUDY
9 × 9⁶

LIVING RM.
15 × 22⁶

BED RM.
12 × 18

C.

DINING RM.
13 × 13⁶

BED RM.
10 × 11

B.

B.

S

L.

C.

C.

C.

C.

BED RM.
12 × 14

C.

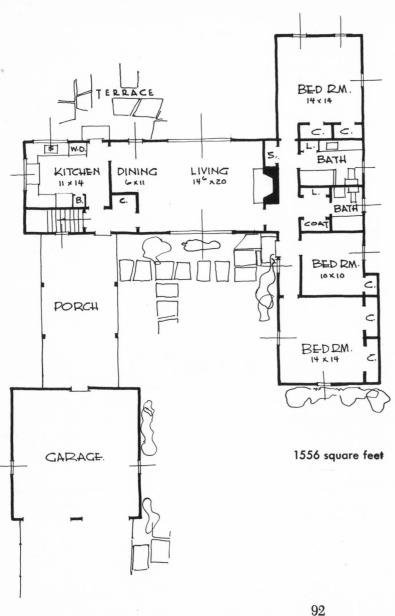

TERRACE

KITCHEN
11 x 14

DINING
6 x 11

LIVING
14⁶ x 20

BED RM.
14 x 14

C.   C.

L.

BATH

L.

BATH

COAT

BED RM.
10 x 10

C.

C.

PORCH

BED RM.
14 x 14

C.

GARAGE.

1556 square feet

By placing the garage toward the street one accomplishes wonders. It gives a short drive for one thing and gives a lot of privacy for another. A fence or a wall tied in with the garage makes for a good outdoor living room.

The combined living room and dining room is delightfully spacious. It's certainly remarkable how we all felt we had to have dining rooms a few years ago and now all-over space seems more important.

There are also three bedrooms and two baths as well as a large basement.

This little house sits snugly on the shore of Kingston Bay just beyond Duxbury, Massachusetts. Since every single dollar counted, nothing was wasted. The living room window was placed to get a lovely vista over the bay. From the dining space the view was shut off by trees so a stock window was used.

Due to the fact that high tides made a basement impossible, a utility room was substituted. It's quite possible to have a cellar in this house by putting stairs in the utility space. There's a lot of attic space too and an additional bedroom may be put in upstairs.

The friendly living kitchen is delightfully cozy and homelike. Old doors and wide board floors were used to carry out the old-time feeling. It's good looking and it functions remarkably well.

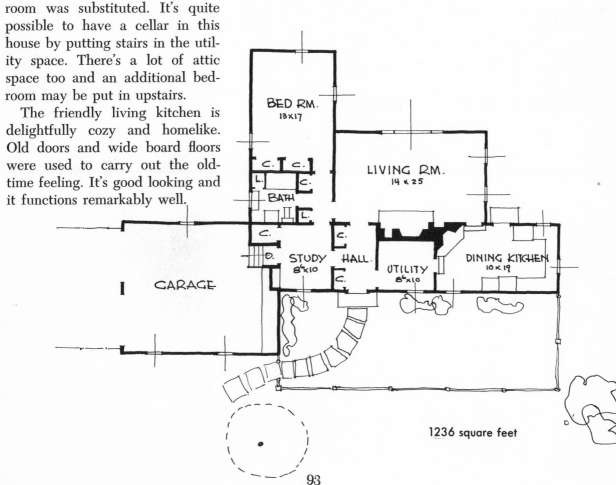

1236 square feet

93

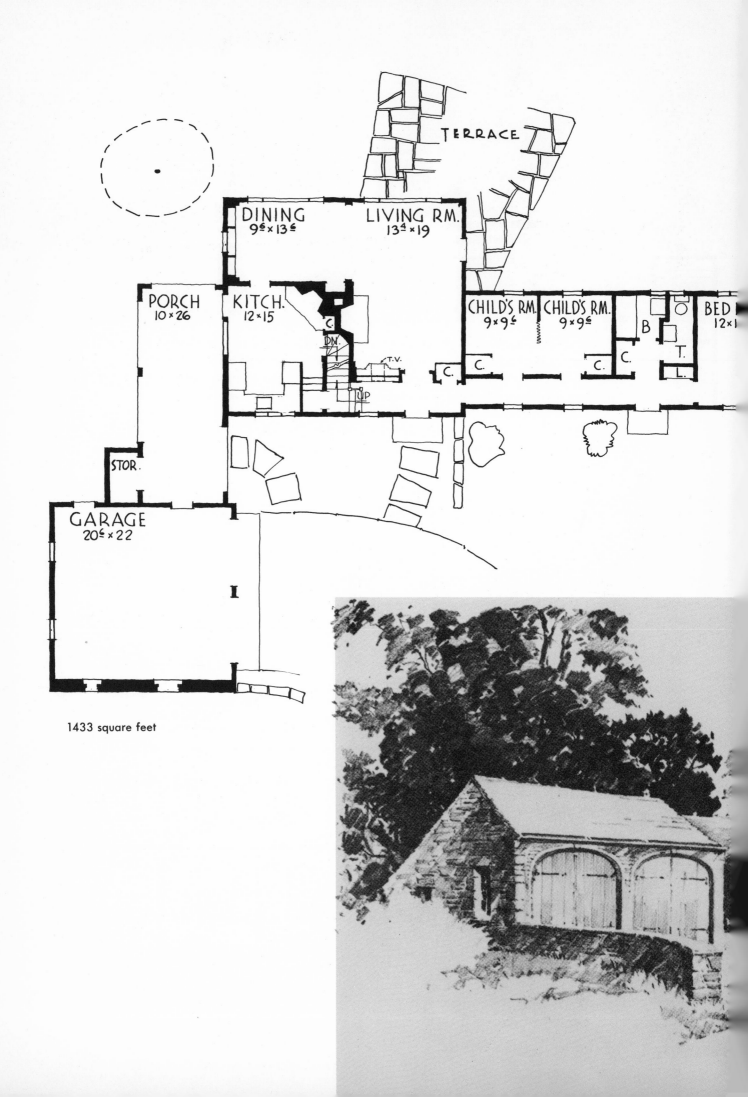

TERRACE

DINING
9⁶×13⁶

LIVING RM.
13⁴×19

PORCH
10×26

KITCH.
12×15

C
DN.

T.V.

UP

CHILD'S RM.
9×9⁶

CHILD'S RM.
9×9⁶

C.

C.

B

BED
12×1

C.

C.

T.

L.

STOR.

GARAGE
20⁶×22

1433 square feet

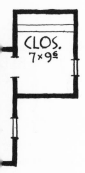

This house with its minute personal scale is charming and proud of it.

Although it may be heir to a Cape Cod house it's no copy book reproduction of it—just a free-wheeling interpretation of it. Its long wings stretch out at right angles like a carpenter's square. It has three bedrooms and a combination bath. The bath can handle twice the load of a single bath. Note that the two children's rooms can be thrown into one if need be.

There's a new state of affairs in the kitchen. Apparently if cooking's going to be work you might as well make fun out of it. If cooking's to be fun we might as well make a family room out of the kitchen. This one with its fireplace and paneled wall is just as livable as any living room. It won't be long before the kitchen is the most expensive room in the house. As a matter of fact I guess with all its equipment it already is.

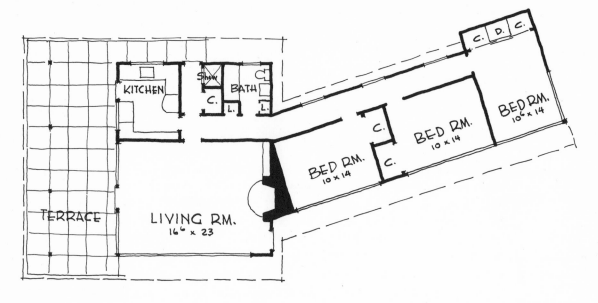

1371 square feet

Most criticisms of contemporary houses are that they are clinical, stripped and dull-looking. This house demonstrates just the opposite. It's light, graceful and imaginative.

The slightly butterflied roof gives it a look of resting lightly on the ground. It's frankly a summer house which explains the location of the bath for maximum use from out of doors. Its windows overlook the broad Atlantic at East Gloucester.

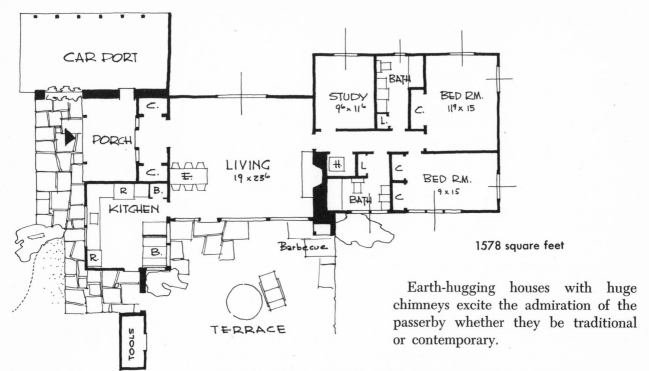

CAR PORT

PORCH

KITCHEN

LIVING
19 x 23⁶

STUDY
9⁶ x 11⁶

BATH

BED RM.
11⁹ x 15

BED RM.
9 x 15

BATH

Barbecue

TERRACE

TOOLS

1578 square feet

Earth-hugging houses with huge chimneys excite the admiration of the passerby whether they be traditional or contemporary.

Whereas most box-like modern houses frequently draw rabid criticism from the layman, a house like the one shown above should delight the eye of even the most traditional-minded.

The whacking big window in the living room opens out on a walled terrace which gives it complete privacy. This kind of a house calls for a lot of glass used discreetly, as it is in this case.

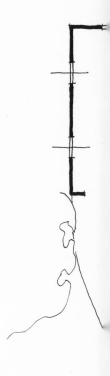

This strung-out little house overlooks a lovely garden and beyond it the blue ocean. The theory behind the plan was to take full advantage of the view and also the south sun which was on the opposite side of the house. Through ventilation was extremely important because the days are hot although the evenings are cool. The house is constructed of pine boards inside and out, well insulated. This makes use of the structural strength of the pine.

The exterior is painted a lavender grey about the color of the ledge on which the house is built. At present there is no plaster in the house. The entire interior is made of rugged beams with pine board ceilings. Most all of the pine is native cut in the vicinity. Floors are of wide boards. The fireplace wall is paneled with old doors painted bright blue and rubbed over with burnt umber. The two ends of the owner's bedroom are also covered with old paneling painted barn red. The ledge is covered with sedum and rock flowers and serves as a sheltered spot in the sun, shielded by the wings of the house.

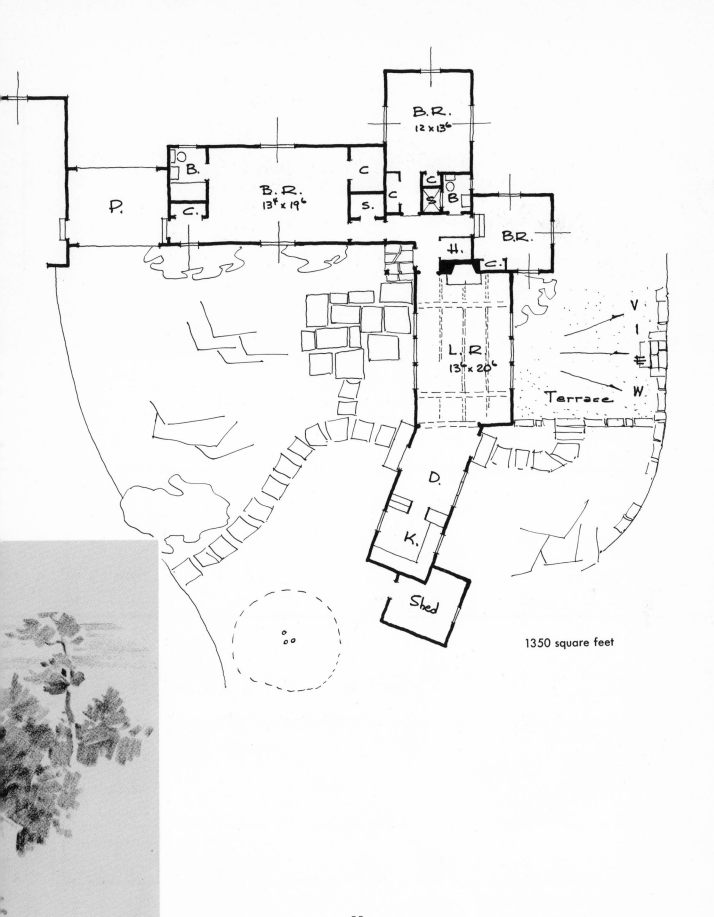

B.

P.

B. R.
13⁴ x 19⁶

C.

B. R.
12 x 13⁶

C

S.

C

C

C

B

B. R.

H.

C.

L. R.
13⁴ x 20⁶

V
I
E
W

Terrace

D.

K.

Shed

1350 square feet

This house is long, low and swanky in the colonial manner. The 'T' shaped plan has excellent circulation and functions smoothly. It's a little house or a big house according to how you look at it. It's almost transitional in style. It has three bedrooms and two baths as well as a living room and big combination kitchen and dining space.

TERRACE

BED RM.
14 x 14

GARAGE

PORCH

LIVING RM.
14 x 20

KITCHEN
10 x 16⁴

BATH

BATH

S.

BED RM.
10 x 10

BED RM.
14 x 14

1422 square feet

100

This colonial ranch house combines all the benefits of both types. It has the economical double-hung windows together with a large window in the living room. A good compact plan, it has excellent possibilities for expansion since there is ample room on the top floor for more rooms if necessary. It has a complete living room and a dining room which is separated by a space divider. The study may be used as a third bedroom.

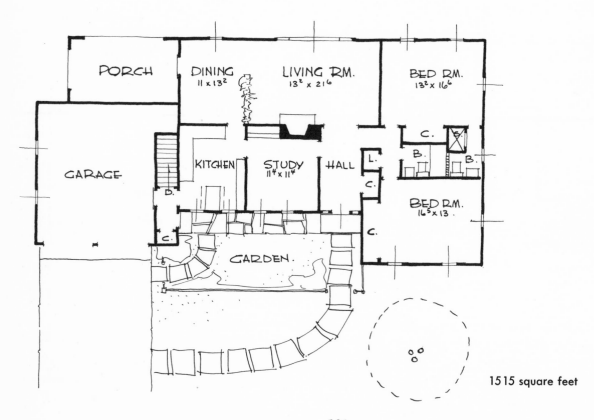

PORCH

DINING
11 x 13²

LIVING RM.
13² x 21⁶

BED RM.
13² x 16⁶

GARAGE

KITCHEN

STUDY
11⁴ x 11⁴

HALL

L.

C.

C.

B.

B.

C.

BED RM.
16⁵ x 13 .

GARDEN.

C.

1515 square feet

101

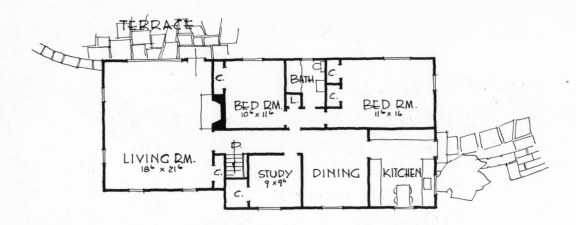

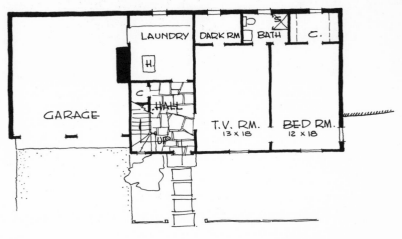

This is a most versatile house. It is large. It can be used as a one-story house or a two-story house. The upper level can be used as one apartment and the lower level for another.

One enters a flagstone-floored hall on the lower level. This has pine walls and a beamed ceiling. Going directly to the upper floor we have a big living room of almost 400 sq. ft. Then there are two bedrooms and bath and a study, dining room and kitchen.

2386 square feet

To return to the lower floor, one finds a large family or TV room and a bedroom and bath and large walk-in closet as well as a small kitchenette or dark room as required. The laundry works in well with the heater room.

Family rooms are quite in vogue. They serve as dining rooms, second living rooms, play rooms, television rooms and all round recreation rooms. Here the kitchen opens directly into the family room. The only separation is a high counter.

A buffet bar serves directly into the alcove in the living room which may also be used for dining.

The flagstone floor in the hall is good for muddy feet and the ten-foot-long coat closet will provide for a big family. This house was designed for a family with three children and a maid. We never call a maid's room by that name because we don't expect the maids to stay very long and it might be bad luck.

There are four baths in this house strategically placed between bedrooms. The study and the living room open onto a whopping living terrace—a big house by present-day standards with lots of living in it.

3187 square feet

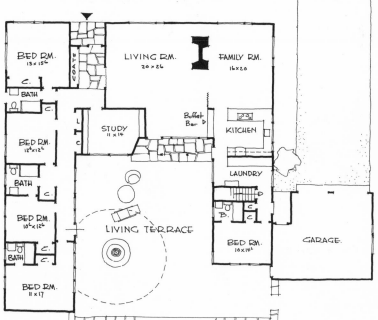

103

This house on a hilltop has lovely views which explains to some extent the odd angle of the living room. Possibilities for outdoor living are excellent with easy serving to the porch and terrace.

The hall has a plant box under the window which narrows in width as you approach the living room door, actually large enough for a small conservatory. There are plenty of good closets as well as a duo bath. The living room is exceptionally large and open to the beamed rafters.

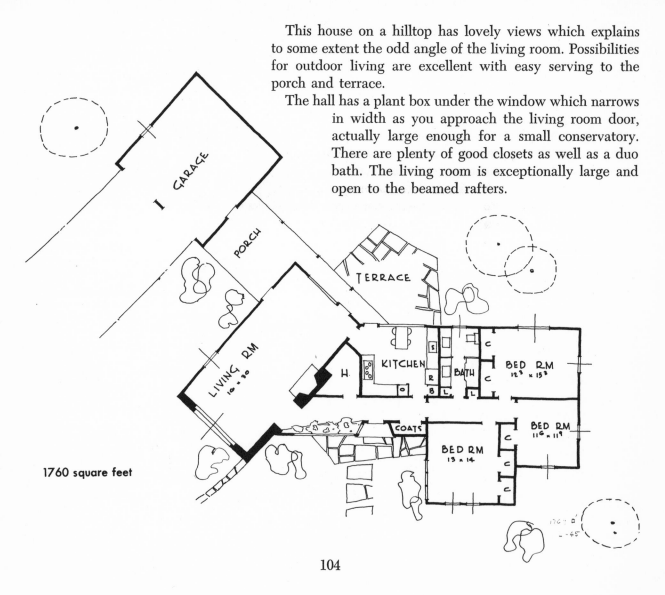

1760 square feet

104

When we started this book we didn't plan to put in any Cape Cod houses but we find that despite the popularity of the so-called ranch house the Cape cottage house still has an immense appeal.

Too many people are liable to associate the Cape Cod house with the typical story and one half plan with labor-making dormers so hard to build in today's mass production market.

This house however is all on one floor and although there is plenty of chance to get to the second floor by means of a stair, there are no finished rooms on the second floor at the present time. It's an easy-living house and it looks big.

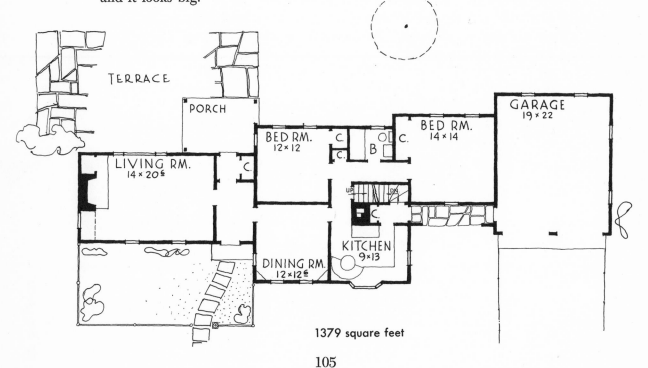

1379 square feet

105

This house of Mr. and Mrs. B. F. Kraus, located on the shore of Buzzards Bay at Falmouth, also graces the cover of this publication. It has that long low ground-hugging look of the really good contemporary house.

Its broad expanse of glass on the ocean side takes in the blue waters of the bay. On the road side the windows are narrow and high to give desired privacy but create cross-draft. On the road side where the windows are small the overhang is small too, for economy's sake. On the water side, where the windows are big, the overhang is wide to shut off the rays of the summer sun.

This house is one room deep to catch the breezes and the view. We always try to give each room a good view on a seaside house.

This house was built in two sections, the main house to the end of the laundry being built first and the garage and small guest room at a later date. Although it is a year-round house, the accent is on summer living so that terrace and barbecue are used a lot.

The trick angle of the garage is not trick at all. It just follows parallel to the lot line as required by building restrictions and every inch of space was required to get in two cars. Originally a one-car garage was planned.

The walls of the house are of pecky cypress and exactly match the color of the old piling at the water's edge.

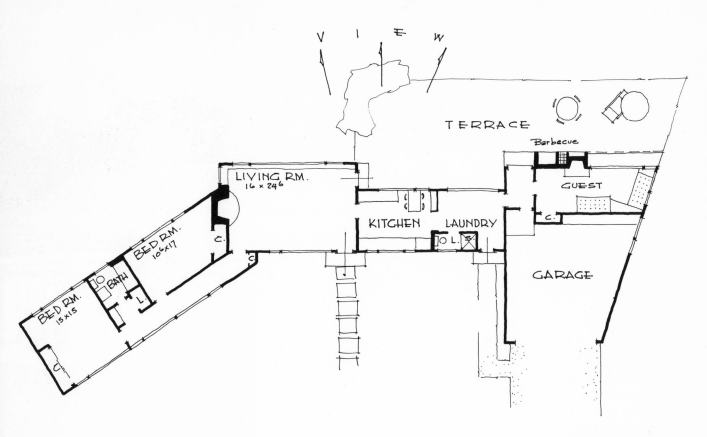

V I E W

TERRACE

Barbecue

LIVING RM.
16 x 24⁶

GUEST

KITCHEN

LAUNDRY

C.

BED RM.
10⁶ x 17

C.

L.

GARAGE

BATH

BED RM.
15 x 15

C.

1665 square feet

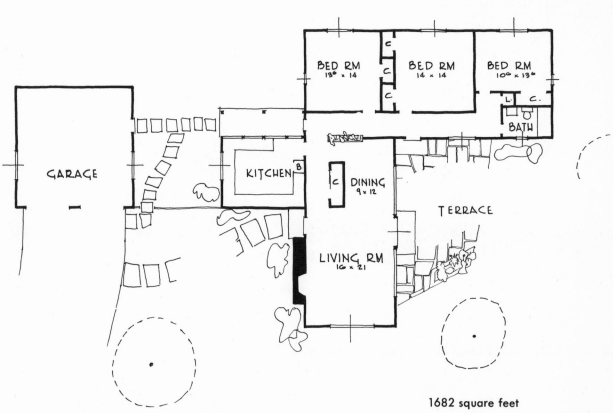

GARAGE

KITCHEN

BED RM
13⁶ × 14

BED RM
14 × 14

BED RM
10⁶ × 13⁶

BATH

DINING
9 × 12

LIVING RM
16 × 21

TERRACE

1682 square feet

This transitional-style house is one which can not be picked out of any book of architectural history. It's emotionally satisfying and comfortably up to date. Made of stone and batten boarding painted white, it will delight the eye of the observer.

This was intended as a vacation house but can easily be used year round. This is a good kind of a house for people who like to have their cake and eat it too. They want good-looking houses and modern conveniences.

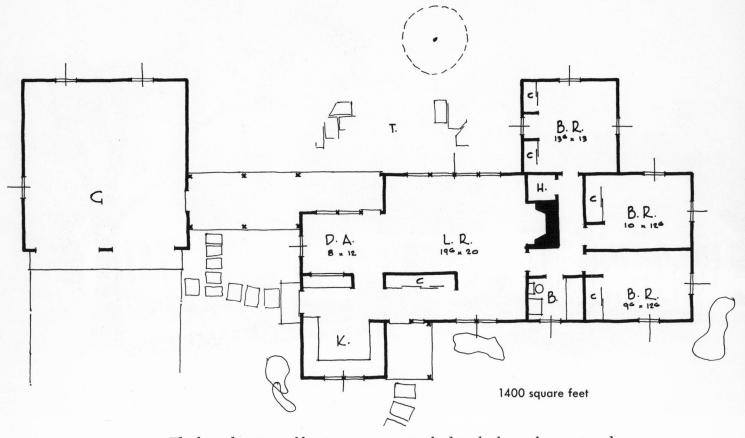

G

T.

D. A.
8 x 12

L. R.
19⁶ x 20

K.

B. R.
19⁶ x 13

H.

B. R.
10 x 12⁶

B.

B. R.
9⁶ x 12⁶

C

1400 square feet

The big advantage of having a garage attached to the house by a covered way rather than blanketing one side of the house is that no windows are blocked out and there is no loss of cross ventilation. The disadvantage of course is the extra cost due to the extra wall needed. It's a great arrangement for attaining privacy and for shielding a terrace for outdoor living and dining.

The outside of this house is made of natural cedar or cypress boards. The windows toward the street are small but those at the rear of the living room and dining area are large.

Here is a house that telescopes easy living. It is easy to build because of the lean-to forms. The main part was built for a summer home with kitchen, living room and bath. The bedroom wing will be added later. Its open plan from the kitchen through sliding doors to the terrace and porch make it truly a house for gracious living.

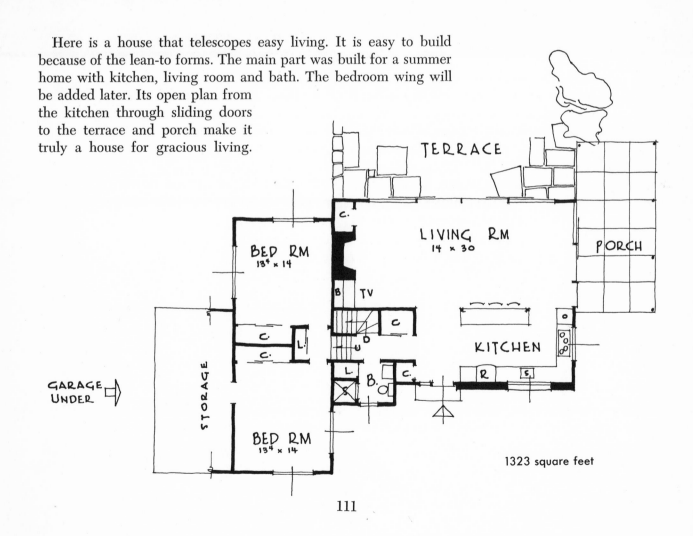

1323 square feet

Trying to get words to describe this sort of a house is not easy. It's elongated and it rambles—I suppose you might say it perambulates.

It has a little bit of history in its background but it speaks with no particular accent. The garage at an odd angle gives it character and the stone terrace wall ties in with the stone chimney and makes the house fit the ground.

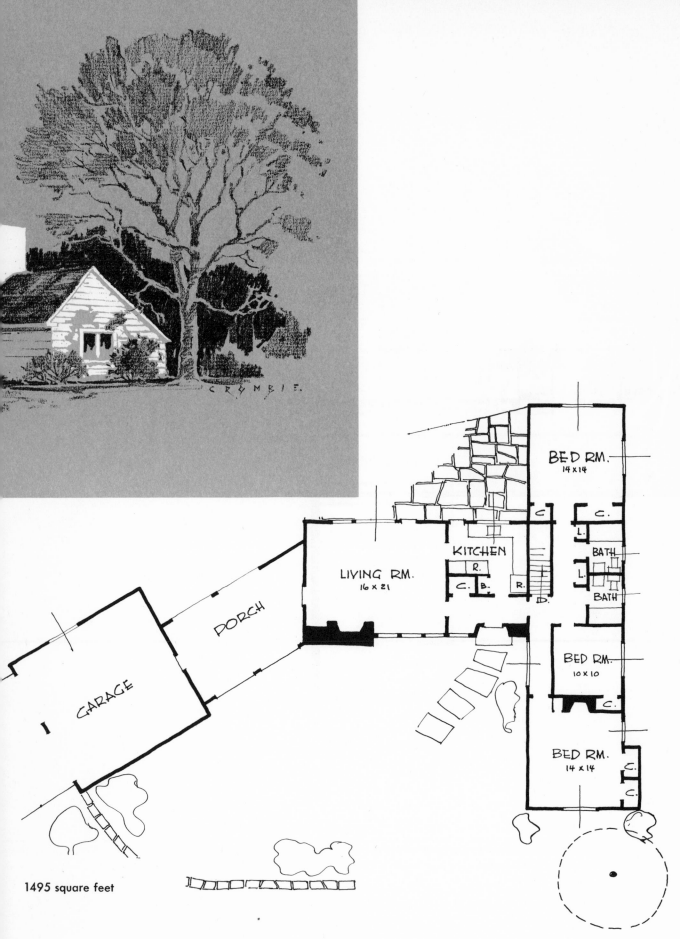

CROMBIE.

BED RM.
14 x 14

C.

C.

L.

BATH

L.

KITCHEN

R.

BATH

LIVING RM.
16 x 21

C. B.

R.

D.

BED RM.
10 x 10

C.

PORCH

GARAGE

BED RM.
14 x 14

C.

C.

1495 square feet

113

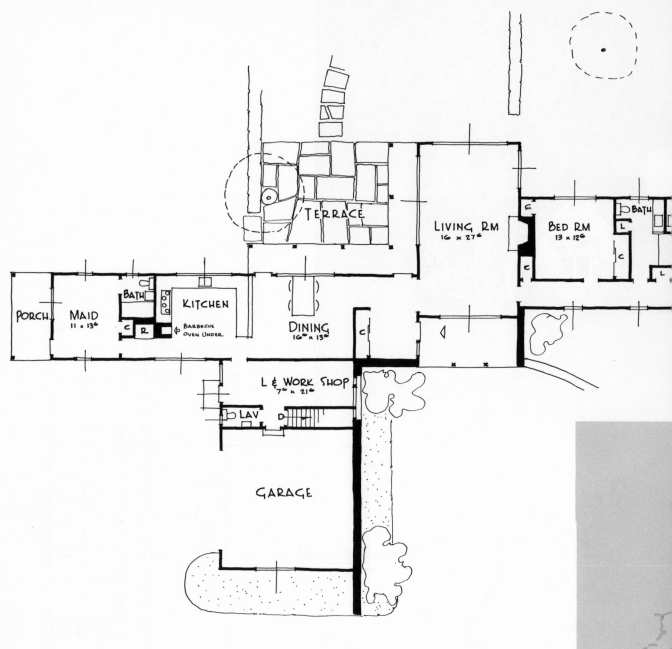

TERRACE

LIVING RM
16 x 27⁶

BED RM
13 x 12⁶

BATH

PORCH

MAID
11 x 13⁶

BATH

KITCHEN

Barbecue
Oven Under

DINING
16⁶ x 13⁶

L & WORK SHOP
7⁶ x 21⁶

LAV

GARAGE

2505 square feet

114

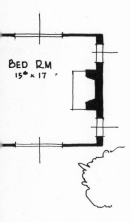

BED RM
15° x 17'

Too many houses are called ranch houses that are no more nor less than made over bungalows of the 1915 period. It's hard to call a square block of a house a ranch house when the true ranch house was generally one room deep and rambled all over the place.

This house has all the features of a true ranch house with its almost pinwheel plan and ells extending in four directions. The large windows take advantage of sweeping views. There's a perfectly marvelous living-kitchen and a wonderfully large living room. The house is well filled with fireplaces, having one in the living room, one in the study and one in the bedroom as well as a barbecue fireplace in the living-kitchen.

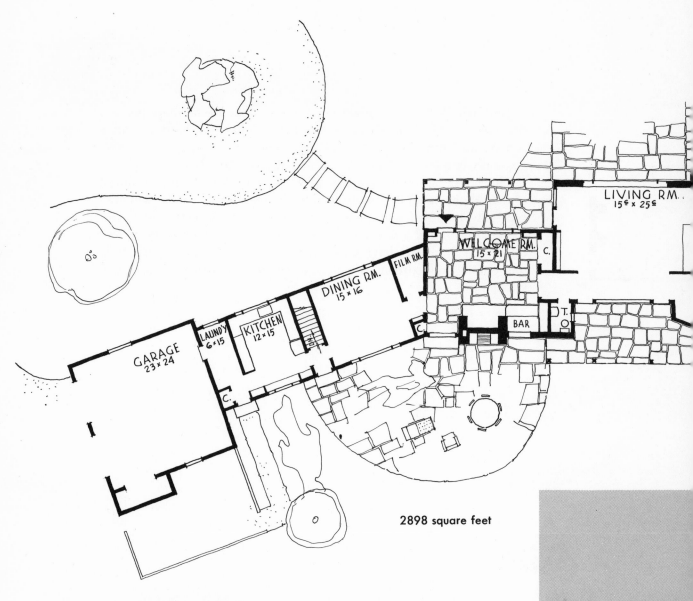

LIVING RM.
15⁶ x 25⁶

WELCOME RM.
15 x 21

C.

FILM RM.

DINING RM.
15 x 16

BAR

T.

C.

KITCHEN
12 x 15

LAUND'Y
6 x 15

GARAGE
23 x 24

C.

2898 square feet

These were the original sketches of the Allard M. Graves house in White River Junction, Vermont. The finished structure is slightly different but the spirit is the same.

One enters the flagstone-floored welcome room with its mammoth stone fireplace and beamed ceiling. The handy bar makes entertaining easy. Mr. Graves, who is in the moving picture business, has many reels of marvelous film and enjoys showing them to his friends so there is a special film room.

116

With panoramic views in all directions, the windows are placed to take advantage of them.

The exterior is of carefully selected quarry stone with rough sawn pine siding stained and whitewashed and then brushed off.

This irregular roofed house faces on a river at Great Barrington, Rhode Island. Designed for two people, it takes advantage of the views without sacrifice of privacy.

The exterior is of natural shale stone found locally and hand split shingles. The roof is of grey-green slate. The house is painted to sympathize with the color of the roof. The barn peak over the windows on the water side shuts out the summer sun while letting the rays of the winter sun enter.

A good example of the way old and new may be combined is the use of old ships' knees and hand hewn posts adjacent to large plate glass windows.

The living room and dining room is finished in teak with a natural stone fireplace in the living room.

The little garden terrace toward the water is a feature.

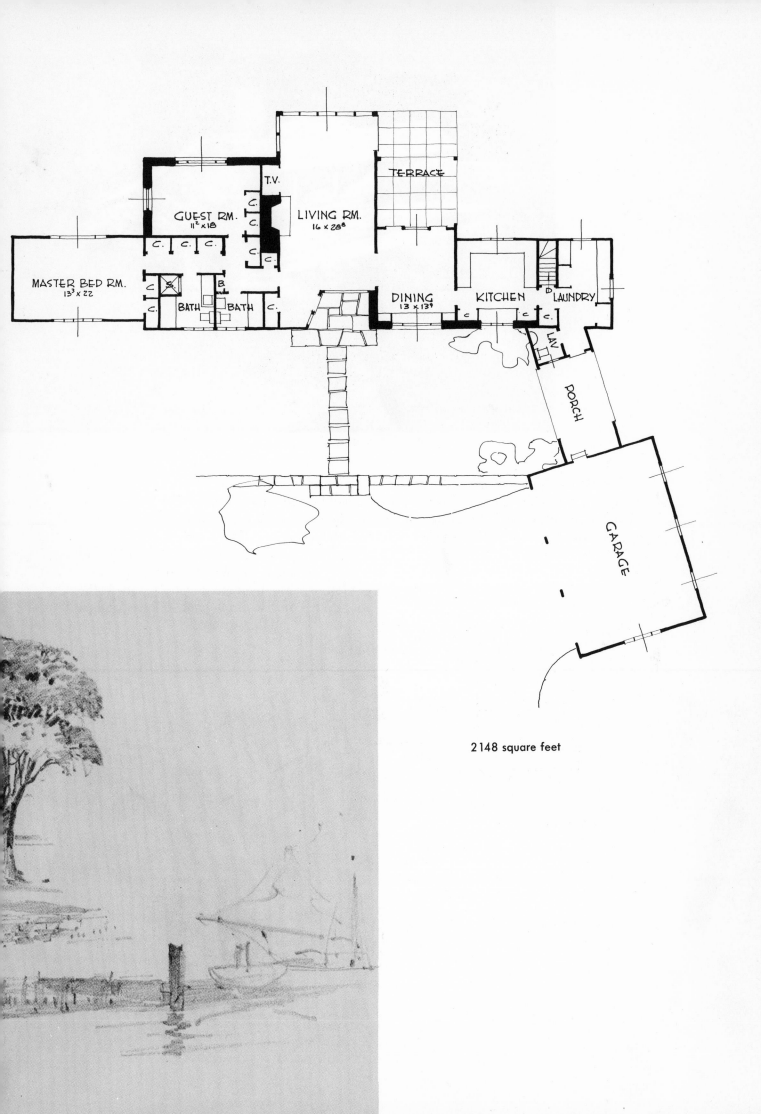

MASTER BED RM.
13³ x 22

GUEST RM.
11² x 18

T.V.

LIVING RM.
16 x 28⁸

TERRACE

C.
C.
C.
C.
C.
C.
C.

C.
BATH
B.
BATH
C.

C.

DINING
13 x 13⁹

KITCHEN

D
LAUNDRY

C.
C.
C.

LAV.

PORCH

GARAGE

2148 square feet

Traditional on the outside and modern on the inside might describe this house. To make the house look informal and rambling the living room is placed at an angle with the sleeping quarters. The spacious living-kitchen is a feature with its fireplace, paneled walls and beamed ceiling. The wood is left natural and the equipment made as inconspicuous as possible. The big dining-living terrace at the rear works in well with the kitchen and dining areas.

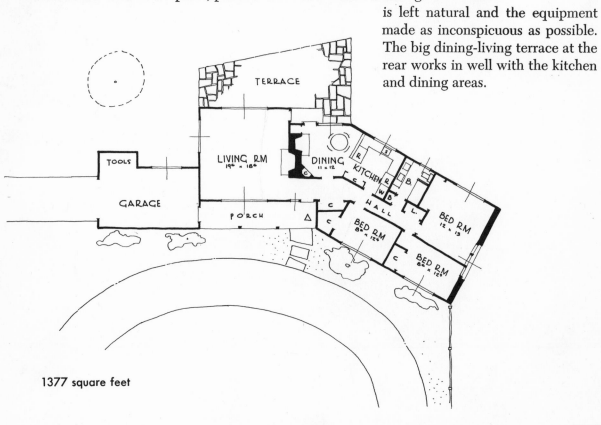

1377 square feet

120